BY WAY OF ART

BY WAY OF ART

CRITICISMS OF MUSIC, LITERATURE,
PAINTING, SCULPTURE, AND THE DANCE

BY
PAUL ROSENFELD

Essay Index Reprint Series

BOOKS FOR LIBRARIES PRESS, INC.
FREEPORT, NEW YORK

First Published 1928
Reprinted 1967

LIBRARY OF CONGRESS CATALOG NUMBER:
67-30230

PRINTED IN THE UNITED STATES OF AMERICA

To
HERBERT J. SELIGMANN

NOTICE

The author is obliged to the editors of The Dial, The Saturday Review of Literature, The New Republic, The New York Evening Post's Literary Review, The New York Evening Sun's bookpage, and Simon and Schuster, publishers of The Pamphlet Poets, for permitting him to clarify, enlarge and revive those of these little penetrations *by way of art* which were first summed up in their friendly columns. They have been left standing in the order in which they were essayed.

CONTENTS

		PAGE
The Woman in the Box	. . . .	1
Thanks to the International Guild: A Musical Chronicle	. . . .	12
1. Preamble	. . . .	12
2. Renard	. . . .	15
3. Les Noces	. . . .	21
4. We Question Strawinsky	. . . . .	26
5. "Igor, tu n'est qu'un villain!"	. . . .	36
6. Hindemith	. . . .	45
7. The Bloch Concerto Grosso	. . . .	53
8. Schoenberg and Varèse	. . . . .	58
9. Rudhyar	. . . .	65
10. Ruggles	. . . .	73
11. Cowell	. . . .	77
12. Szymanowski's Case	. . . . . .	80
13. Buhlig Integrates	. . . . . .	85
14. Arcanes	. . . .	89
15. Remembering Florence Mills	. . . .	94
El Greco's Portrait of Himself	. . . . .	99
The Place of Gertrude Stein	. . . . .	111

CONTENTS

	PAGE
THE LETTERS OF MADAME MÈRE DU REGENT	132
HEMINGWAY'S PERSPECTIVE	151
AN AMERICAN SONNETEER: DONALD EVANS	164
THE CITY: WITH A GLANCE AT HONEGGER	174
EMANUEL CARNEVALI'S BOOK	186
SCULPTURE BY GASTON LACHAISE	198
THE DANCE OF ANGNA ENTERS	209
TURNING TO AMERICA: THE CORN DANCE	217
THE IMPORTANCE OF RICHARD ALDINGTON	236
SACRED AND PROFANE MUSIC	250
"VOGEL ALS PROPHET": ALFRED KREYMBORG	258
COPLAND WITHOUT THE JAZZ	266
THE AMERICANISM OF CARLOS CHAVEZ	273
THE PAGANISM OF WALLACE GOULD	284
WHY DO I WRITE?	304

BY WAY OF ART

THE WOMAN IN THE BOX

WHEN the opportunity of returning murderer-
wise to the scene of so many of my crimes was offered me, the musical appetite was spry as usual in
early autumn; and the discovery there was no two-
hand literature about, a sharp disappointment. The
volumes in the cabinet of the friends who had
kindly loaned me their baby-grand for an afternoon, called exclusively for the duet of violin and
piano. I dare say my friends believed I played by
heart, I who have never been able to memorize a
phrase. Fortunately, I remembered having come
upon a score of Tannhäuser in the attic; fetched it
without much enthusiasm; and, turning the pages
of the old volume, began with the stringed passage
in the second act which immediately follows upon
the triumphal entry of the Hofbräu guests. As I
played, and my delight at the recovery of something
as good as the lyrical page grew with each bar, a
curious realization came to me. (Summers are truly
fecund seasons for musical scribes. Musical rou-
tine is far, leaving spirit free to seize the moment.)

Everyone knows the graceful tune in G accompanying the entrance of the band of minnesingers into the Landgraf's feudal hall. Sustained music for the gradual strings, it constitutes one of the many colored "evening stars" of the old-fashioned opera. The chromatic melody swings at moderate speed with lyrical trills over abrupt march-like chords, across unexpected intervals and through sweet unpredictable progressions. The romantic lyre is in these elegant, fervent tones of lightly mystical aspiration, the poet's sense of painful election, the ceremonial pride and fire of the youthful Wagner summoned to his rôle. A brief development section brings the initial phrase in reiterated movements of balanced ascension and regression, till, in a climax soft and deliberate as the curl of a summer wave, an appoggiatura of the submedian arrests, gathers and holds the surge; and sets the music slowly diminishing in the serene maintenance of the perfect moment; sustained, noble and relaxed as the gesture of a muse. And, if not to every one, at least to most people who play the piano, there must be known the experience of hearing, while their fingers rest upon the keyboard, a human voice speak out from the polished case where but a moment since percussion vibrated; a voice both the sound of the mechanism and of an human throat; an expressive bodily tone fading very quickly in the conscious moment, while the sound again becomes the normal tone of flat ringing stones and struck copper wires. This was the phenomenon which once again startled me while I sat pleased with the unfamiliar quality of my friends' piano and the grace of the rediscovered bit. There it was again, incomprehensible apparition, sudden corporeality of the most impalpable of mediums, a woman speaking inside the black box, low and distinctly through the exalted melody. I say melody, as if all the elements of the music had not instantaneously been merged in the sound of a woman murmuring intimately, fervently in beauty; as if something more satisfying had not for a fleeting minute replaced them, sustaining nonetheless perfectly the material flow through time. What made this brief harmless illusion particularly memorable, was the unusual circumstance that the murmuring from the black case came so distinctly through the pianistic tone that it related itself, in my imagination, to a definite form and look and condition of corporeity. The other voices had evoked the sense of presences, too. But they had been wraithlike; while this rose before my mind decided for all its bluish fluidity, and compulsive like an object of sense. The musical lines seemed lightly delineating a bust and throat and a head wreathed with hair, and there finding fulfillment. The woman took the music into herself. Still music, it turned into her. She smiled where it was.

The illusion could not have lasted longer than a brief two seconds. Yet in that small fraction of time I had grown fully conscious of a look simultaneously spiritual, passionate, permeated by an ideal longing. (The individual traits were felt more than seen, but with astonishing clearness.) From underneath the eyelids came a thrilling blue light, alive with yearning for a thing finer, more intense and filled with fire of the ghost than what is usually found on earth, or has been found unto this day. Of all it fell upon it seemed to demand transfigured flesh, incorporate spirit. Perfectly aware that I had not seen its source before, for the woman resembled no one I had hitherto met, I nonetheless knew she was not strange to me, no stranger than the familiar music realizing her trait on trait. Something in me had long been semi-conscious of her, as of a resident of the next city block casually glimpsed a few times from distances. At last I had met her,

[4]

unpreparedly as one finds such neighbors at a party. But in this encounter there was torment as well as fun. . . . The gripping moment passed. Just as I felt the air of another period, the middle nineteenth century about her coiffure and dress, and an old-fashioned spirit in the regard of summoning, smiling, inspiring eyes in which two glow-worms shone, they were gone, become memories merely. Nonetheless, I was aware now who she was and where I had known her. About me there leaped like the flame-tongues of bonfires, the musical style, the poetic ˙message, the symbolism and spirit of Wagner's art; filled with new interest but felt entirely in terms of her. The chromatic, aspiring element of Wagner's musical writing, the ideal longing: what was it but an approximation of her expression of countenance; and she but the archi-type of his characteristic soaring, penetrative tone? Yes; she was the woman who had moved and haunted the composer all his life with her look of waiting! I knew her, at last: Wagner's woman, the one whose presence is felt throughout his art; wait-ing; her being taut in tender, almost painful watch-ing for the unknown comer. . . . The one whom he intended when he said that each of his dramatic

[5]

actions embodied the relationship of the same pair of people, endlessly continued. Figured in different instances as Senta and Sieglinde, Elsa and Kundry, the sleeping Brünnhilde and the Brünnhilde with Siegfried's ring, her spirit is felt not only when the curtain is up on the scene and the action unfolds. Where there is no scene, the music is full of her; certain interludes, notably the second in the first act of Götterdämerung, materially evoking her. For years before that moment in the sitting room of my friends, Wagner's art had been making her known to me, hinting her, shadowing her forth, showing me her traits in fluid impalpable form; and what it had all been about, the marvelous music, was simply her mysterious self!

Wagner's woman! But whom did those words signify, I began asking myself in the days that followed; half knowing they meant no particular person, but moved to give the practical interpretations a hearing. Was the figure I had seen Minna Planer, Mathilda Wesendonck, Cosima Liszt? Or were the rigorous psychoanalysts: the ones who profess to hold that the greater the complex, the greater the resulting art, to be credited; and was she indeed Wagner's mother; and the pose of attendance in which he saw her the image of his

[6]

mother waiting upon the birth of the posthumous child that he had been? Or was she merely his own slightly oversoft nature? This interpretation was the first to go. The goody in the man invariably is an inferior affair, just as the man in the woman invariably is a low-class tom, jealous, as intolerant of knowledge surpassing his own as a longshoreman; and the rare presence manifested me was filled with the upward impulse of a muse. The other explanation I found equally shallow. Had Wagner been fixated on one woman, mother or sister, of which fixation this brooding presence was the sign, the influence of more than a single woman could scarcely have succeeded in establishing itself in his life; and that, we know, was profoundly stirred by passions. No; it seemed much more likely that the mother and Minna, Mathilda and Cosima, were all of them the archi-typical woman; rathermore than she any single one of them. For what I really had been made to feel and know in the penetrant moment, was that she was a picture or form older in Wagner than his experience of any individual, and merely matched and fulfilled by his mother and the other fateful women.

Attentive of a new element in the world, what was the secret Wagnerian woman but the rib of the man, the ideal complement intuition of whom every one brings into the world with him: the well-nigh cosmic object each strives to realize for himself out of quick material, calling to, struggling toward like Siegfried through the fire, and expiring in, like Tristan in Isolde's arms? A Platonic Idea, surely; for what were the Ideas of Plato but spirit-lovers of the soul? For the male, ideas of this sort remain referable to particular feminine types; and yet to see in these mystic objectives mere sexual goals is vulgarly to misconceive them. No doubt but for Richard Wagner the idea was at one time Mathilda and at another Cosima. Yet it was equally simply the dramatic fictions Elizabeth and Isolde, Venus and Eva Pogner; and beyond them, a spirit pervading his entire world-picture, storms and seas, forest deeps and midsummer evenings, heroic loves and deaths. As I conceived it, it was indeed everything seen and heard of Wagner in terms of the phenomenal and the evanescent; everything compulsive of work; and transmuted by the effort to seize it in its diverse manifestations, and satisfy upon it eternally reborn desire into not only the action but the musical style of his dramas.

Nonetheless, it was a woman of flesh. While it

would be inept to see in the motive merely the female, it would be equally inept not to recognize its basic connection with her. An individual was the hidden agent; perhaps the person glimpsed by me. With a certain comfort, I remembered the Old Testament's assurance that the Mother of All the World was Eve: the mother of the world as Will and as Idea; knowing that Schopenhauer and Wagner both would so have understood it, too; and recollecting that the Hebrew word Eve was the symbol of the feminine sex. The material fount of the world; simultaneously its bourne. Once again I recognized the significance of the fact that it was a piece of music written for performance during the entrance of the musician-poets, men in whom Wagner must have felt himself, which had been instrumental in revealing me his ideal partner. It was for "Elizabeth" these troubadours were to sing, it was before her they were bowing; and in creating the atmosphere of their train and expressing the impulse of their rivalry and the high poetic function and tournament of love, Wagner had bodied forth the unconscious matrix of his own activity: the material woman to whose new psychophysical quality his work brought the response. Life during

the nineteenth century had produced a refined,
highly pitched feminine type awaiting the man capable of feeling life with the sensitivity and elevation necessary to release her; and in producing
many artists capable of deliverance, it had produced one pre-eminently able to feel the world-
whole in magically complementary fashion; and in
him, the germ of Wagner's career and music.

Later, I wondered whether the art had come any
the closer for the discovery? Or whether the little
anatomy had weakened its hold. No, it had neither
come nearer to me nor withdrawn. It still affected
me as "magnificent music." But life itself, the unformed mass of experience seemed firmer for the
discovery. There was a fine excitement in perceiving the direct relationship between all innovations,
developments and intensifications of artistic style
of the revolutionary nature of Wagner's, with obscure mutations in the human plasm announcing
themselves in new somatic expressions, new gestures, looks and tones of voice; and demanding new
sensitivities and acutenesses, new qualities of inter-
course, on the part of the sexes. Sensitive, passionate, spiritual women then had always grown conscious of themselves and found their emotional
forms through the works of artists! Art built a sort

of bridge; the need of bridges between women and men was strong at the great multiple root of art! Form itself was determined largely by the looks of living people, was born of the ideal corporeal complements of poets, composers, painters, critics. Musicians found their points of contact more in the unconsciously apprehended tones of the voice, painters in the gestures and facial expressions of the new feminine types; all the artists commencing with some one aspect of the new nervous body, and referring to it again the whole of life felt by them. Our own times were busy throwing their bridges. If indeed our day was strongly artistic and ambiguous in its art, typified by The Waste Land, Ulysses and À La Recherche du Temps Perdu, it nonetheless had artists of the directness of Lawrence, Stieglitz, Lachaise; and the added incitement of a femininity declaring itself to the man. . . . For a single moment, doubt again dampened my discoverer's joy, as I recollected the Frenchman's *plus ça change, plus c'est la même chose.* Was the situation ever new? Another moment assented. It was always new and terrible and wonderful on the high seas of life; and great artists found their native motion only where the Atlantic smiles and storms, and the swells are broadest.

[11]

THANKS TO THE INTERNATIONAL GUILD: A
MUSICAL CHRONICLE

I. PREAMBLE

EDGAR VARÈSE and Carlos Salzedo, operating under
the name, The International Composers' Guild,
maintained a hatchery for musical bacilli where in
glass boxes new combinations and voices, æsthetics
and world-feelings germinated. Twice or thrice a
year doctor and assistant doctor went about their
secret forcing-house examining the queer little
growths and culling those apparently possessing the
power of life. Then a concert was arranged, and
the small experiments let into the world. During
some five years, 1922–1927, these genial musicians
made their periodic deliveries of musical germs; and
so infectious were certain cultures that to-day we
dwell among horizons of art, hence of the world,
thrust back by them. (Again the advantage of permitting creative spirits to conduct artistic organizations stands evident. In the hands of the artist, the institution becomes a means of expression
second only to his own work; another instrument

for the affirmation of his day; the instrumentality of the work of his fellows producing in the
director something of the disinterestedness and
serious approach characterizing high scientific
spheres.)

Like other hatcheries, Varèse and Salzedo's produced its chickens with two heads, its vocalizing
sturgeons and strange composite bugs. The buzz
of life was not unvaryingly strong on the International's Sunday nights in Aeolian Hall, ever the
Cave of Winds. Affirmativeness led the two radicals
to pledge their Guild to discoveries, disclosure of
the new in vision, personality and method; and
since Americas are not to be revealed at will, certain of their releases had a sterile curiosity, a purely
speculative interest. Still, the professional, inquisi-
tive, experimental tension invariably persisted. A
responsiveness to the hour, a spirit of initiative,
promptitude and willingness which we in New
York still tend to associate with Parisian circles,
combined as it was with an artistic standard of
performance, distinguished even the Guild's dull-
est parties from those of rival organizations. The
Society of the Friends of Music declared itself a
musical museum beside the Guild. Pro Arte evidently was another depot for modern French work;

and the League of Composers a social function where the performance of music served the ambitions of mediocrities; handsomely dressed people conversed up and down the aisles; and music preluded to an apotheosis of personal projections and chicken salad in close quarters. Occasionally, the net gain of an International Sunday evening was no more than an amusing suggestion, like the one provided the evening Henry Cowell demonstrated with the amerindian thunder-stick, and found the tone of primitive American godwardness. At other times, it was merely the promise of a new musical geography; as the evening when the program introduced music by a Chilean, an Italian from Crete, a Negro from Mississippi and a Mexican born, bred and resident in the city of Mexico; and the voices and racial backgrounds of Acario Cotapos, Massimo Zanotti-Bianco, William Grant Still and Carlos Chavez queer-colored the musical future. Frequently, the rewards were magnificent and memorable. Many of them, the single concert appearance of little Florence Mills, for example, enshrined their moments. Others, such as the presentations of Les Noces, Renard, Hyperprism and Integrales, and, in second line, the introductions of Ruggles, Hindemith, Rudhyar, Webern and

[14]

Chavez, established new musical values; and were cardinal in producing here in New York an audience capable of receiving a fresh musical expression at the creative moment. Perhaps essentially critical, our time possesses a stomach for art sounder and robuster, a level of taste superior to the last two centuries'; and much of the advance is due to the work of the experimental stations of which 291 Fifth Avenue is perhaps the most, and the International Composers' Guild not the least, important. To review the experiences for which we have to thank the association of Varèse and Salzedo is therefore not only to appreciate a number of the more significant compositions and composers discovered during the last years, and to define the main lines of musical advance. It is also to make the growth in taste, elevatory to planes of subtler, wider understanding, more positive and our own.

2. RENARD

There is a propriety in beginning this little chronicle of recent developments in music with an account of the Strawinsky pieces played by the International Composers' Guild. While it is doubtful whether Stravinsky is a creator and form-finder of

[15]

the first water; and while his most recent, classicizing compositions make us wonder whether he is
not a sort of musical *agent-provacateur*, gaining the
confidence of the creative wing only at the strategic moment to sell out to the stand-patters; there is
no doubt that the recent revulsion from musical
romanticism to humanism was made largely under
his leadership. That of Satie was, after all, more theoretical. The scores Strawinsky produced between
1914 and 1920, beautifully conveyed the new
orientation, the new humanistic conception of the
material of music and its treatment. The composer
of Renard, Les Noces, L'histoire du soldat, the
Symphonies for Wind-Instruments, and other less
ambitious pieces, was eminently one of those gifted
individuals whose personal road coincides with the
general. The direction of human society, with its
new mass-life, communism, impersonality, was par-
alleled by some anti-individualism in his own desires; and the two reacted upon and strengthened
one another. Having begun as an ultraromantic,
descriptive, precious composer influenced by the
Russian romanticism of Rimsky and the aristocratic French romanticism—impressionism—of Debussy, he found himself increasingly uninterested
by that individualistic spirit, its "respiration of

[16]

Bayreuth," jewelry and pictoriality; and increasingly drawn toward dryer, preciser, more absolute musical forms; and moved to relinquish the expression of the singular, the subjective and the remote in favor of the commonplace, the external, even the banal. The general experience was again full of interest: John Smith, and what happened to Mary; and Strawinsky's embodiments of it were more plastic than his great romantic pieces, Petrushka and Le Sacre du Printemps. These had been a trifle too "intellectual," too subservient to the literary conception, wanting the great line and relentless logic. The form was piecemeal, leaning upon the stage. But the new works were more independent; and quite as full as their immediate predecessors of the brilliant ideas, rhythms and colorations, tones of "the moment," which had made Strawinsky the most interesting of living composers.

Renard, the first important Strawinsky composition offered by the Guild, is the first of these expressions of the new humanism. An animal fable for male voices and small orchestra, it represents a complete break with the direction of the romantic past that still held Strawinsky during the time he wrote Petrushka and Le Sacre. Like all revolu-

tionary acts, Renard flowed from tendencies astir
well before the performer's birth. It is fruit of
established tradition, that of the Russian national-
istic school. The Russian Five not only used
demotic musical idioms. All of them, and Moussorgsky in particular, had before them the ideal of
a popular, primitive and robust art, expressive of
the common experiences of humanity and free in
spirit as well as idiom from grandiosity and preciousness. Tolstoy inveighing against the superb,
godlike spirit of Wagner; and setting up as models
of art the bare naïve representations of peasant
fairs, was merely carrying to a fanatical extreme
the essentially communal, humanistic, perhaps even
Christian feeling of Russia. This æsthetic, Strawinsky inherited by temperament and as pupil of
Rimsky-Korsakoff; and we find him embodying it
in several works preceding Renard. Petrushka to a
degree is humanistic, disillusioned, even primitivis-
tic, in Moussorgsky's intention. Its idiom is based
on the musical expressions of the populace, folk
songs and dances and barrel-organ tunes; and the
interlude for snare drum alone is characteristic of
the color of the work, deliberately bunting and
booths, coachmen and nursemaids, concertinas, fifes
and the atmosphere of a gingerbread fair. In Le

[18]

Sacre du Printemps too Strawinsky aimed at a
primitivism; embodying not the modern masses but
the human past; the herd life surviving in man's
unconscious. Here melody, harmony and rhythm
are deliberately brutal, angular, inarticulate, expressive of the human strata where the individual does
not exist, and life is blind instinct and swarm-
being. For all its romanticism Le Sacre is the first
communist ballet. The peculiar tone-color of Renard, the "village band" music for trumpet, cym-
bal and drum opening and closing of the little
farce, and the huzzahing and falsetting of the
singers, therefore are not without grand precedents
in Strawinsky's own art.

What distinguishes Renard from its predecessors, is the fact that it is better formed than they,
and of a healthier temper. Humanistic and disabused in idea, it is self-definitive, and free from
the traces of romanticism and preciousness which
compromise the spirit of the great ballets. Both
Petrushka and Le Sacre lean to a degree on literary
and mimetic ideas for their meanings. Petrushka
is not without descriptivity. Jewelry of a kind, a
love of the singular harmony and the rare color,
flashes through the deliberately humble material.
Besides, the humor is essentially romantic. The pup-

pet hero is a last incarnation of the important, unhoused, romantic ego, while the music expresses the pathos and irony of election and superiority-inferiority. Though Le Sacre embodies a common experience, the common life of man, it seizes upon it in terms of the monstrous and the remote, and by means of a music that points back to the faëry of Rimsky-Korsakoff. The music of Renard nonetheless is as pure in form as in popularity. It is not piecemeal; does not lean on literary or mimetic ideas; and is not descriptive. It merely fixes the general mood of the cruel and comic animal faibleau it embodies. By virtue of its independence it is nonetheless able, even in concert-form, to bathe us in the atmosphere of the rude sideshow, and set us amid the birchbark shoes and red grinning faces of Russian peasants and children. Preciosity is entirely out of the picture. No harmony or instrumental effect calls attention to itself. The rhythms snap and accelerate with a certain ease. Shrill, robust, homely and rough to threadbareness, the music has a uniform and appropriate coloration; recalling both peasant improvizations and the cantatas of Bach, so notably regular in their instrumental hues. The savage humor is free of romantic irony. It is not the Master of the Show, but human nature,

universal nature, that is satirized in the self-com-
placency of the cock sunning himself upon his
perch and caressing himself with his little guardian
doodle-do, in the hypocrisy of mother fox disguised
as a nun and entreating master cock to come down
and be confessed, in the lamentations of the poor
cock in the hands of the crafty wretch, and in the
fatal curiosity of the latter when cat and goat began their serenade. Perhaps Renard is not the greatest Strawinsky. It has the scope of neither Petrushka, Le Sacre, or Les Noces. The musical ideas
are not striking; and there are brittle and even
dull pages among its gleeful, sportive ones. But unlike its predecessors it builds up. And beneath the
savagery, there is much health. Ultimately, it is
health that interests.

3. LES NOCES

Dominant in Renard, the new method triumphed
in Les Noces, with Le Sacre one of the capital pieces
of modern music. Les Noces is humanistic like Renard, but a larger, more powerful and complicated
expression; moving us not with the indirection
and irony, savagery and burlesque of the animal
fable, but with feeling in its simple, immediate

form. This is to say that signori brutality and sentimentality, twin eccentric halves of emotional disconnection, must find the music respectively sac-
charine and cold. The raucous, strident, willful
note is well out of it, and the ungirt, facile unrestrained one out of it as well. But where there is
capacity for direct relation, sensation, emotion and
sentiment, the vibrance must gratify. Indeed, so
justly does the work convey the proportion of robustness and tenderness, impersonality and secret
warmth which inform our best experience, that
one can well have the illusion that Les Noces is "it."

Strawinsky calls from the four pianos and
the little battery a simultaneously metallic, frosty,
and dense quality of sound. Bell tones permeate the
instrumental medium, flat Kremlin chimes, clock
strokes, tzings of Chinese temple gongs: bell tones
always bright, sharp, high up in air, quickly muf-
fled and cut off as peals in Europe on certain
gaudies. A scattering of cloudy pages throws the
robustious brilliance into relief; and the movingly
spaced series of clangorous chords, struck at the
end, seems merely to gather and decisively hold the
firm rich quality of white metals, nickel, silver, and
steel, felt throughout the score.

Reserve, austerity of strength, characterizes the entire medium; the human no less than the instrumental. Chorus and soli sound somewhat as the voices in Renard, clamant, severe, half impersonal, bare of nuances, and with a strangely satisfying liturgical monotony. In section four, the ribald wedding festival, shouted tones of speech and falsetto singing thrust their dry and burlesque timbers into the broad rigid flow, lightening it; but the entire effect is of a running fresco of uniform, loud, lively, not too sensitive hard sound, expressive of whole, unnervous and not too intuitive people.

Frankly conceived as the exploitation of a material, a medium, Les Noces affects us directly as sonority, leaning on no visual or literary idea. It is wholly an expressive play of rigid lines and volumes. None of Strawinsky's pieces, neither Renard nor the Symphonies for Wind Instruments, stands more the object existing outside the artist, in its own right. Here, the music is the action; and, played with a ballet or without one, carries the intent. Various moods traverse it as the ritual of the peasant marriage unfolds, and the bride dresses, the bridegroom leaves his house, the parents relinquish their children and the new couple ceremoniously bed. But the different moods, barbaric gaiety and sadness, tenderness and ribaldry remain structural carriers of the central quality. The very style has the cool fire of objectivity. There is abuse of *ostinato,* but drunken rhythmic stuff, compulsive wild dancebeats and cubic jerks and accents are given, with an elegance Strawinsky has not equaled. The score is clearly, transparently written for all its polyharmony and polyrhythmicality; solid with the telling counterpoint of the later Strawinsky, and cumulative in its effect. No dry rasping passages break the brisk, never precipitous movement of the four conjoined sections, each very slightly larger in volume than the last. The vasty clockstrokes of the solemn conclusion round and resolve the well-sustained initial impulse.

These items distinguish Les Noces from Strawinsky's earlier peak, the intrinsically romantic consecration. The ultimately differentiating trait nonetheless is the fact that Les Noces, unlike the Sacre with its monstrosity of proportion, and fearful feeling of an alien, excessive and tigerish nature, is entirely human in scale. Through it we find ourselves in a world relative and proportionate to man, before a portal not too vasty for him and ad-

justed to his size. This is the region that concerns
him and is his proper study. We hear the voices
of the human being as the drive of sex selection
gives him themes: voices of virginal fear and painful manumission and majoration; ancestral promptings; orgiastic suggestions; tenderness from the untouched depths, and the heart of decision in which
blind transmitted energies gather themselves for a
new thrust into the unknown. We feel Man; and
not, as in Le Sacre, human bacilli, pistons, brain-
less bobbing organisms that dance when power is
applied to them, and make machine-like, involuntary gestures and motions. The humanity whose
impulses are embodied in Les Noces remain a rudimentary, unindividualizing horde. Personality is
not yet present; in any case it is not the individual
aspects of his peasants and people that have interested the composer. Still, the music has a volun-
tariness, a decisiveness, a species of active virtue
different from the fatalistic and passive spirit of
Le Sacre. There, it is the earth that does; fecundating herself with the blood of man. He is scarcely
separated from her; in all things her unconscious
child. In Les Noces there is still a sacrifice and a
death. A man and woman die so that a new life
made of them both may begin. But, still blind, still

half-conscious, man consents. What spirit of choice, concentration, willingness in the series of dire bell-strokes cutting bride and groom off from their past and rounding the piece! *Amor fati!* and with the spirit of consent, choice, selection, freedom and Man are here.

4. WE QUESTION STRAWINSKY

Strawinsky was a good thirty minutes late for rehearsal the afternoon I interviewed him. The handful of musicians assembled for Renard and Ragtime sat or strolled languidly about on the atticky bare stage of Carnegie Hall. The horn player amused himself by blowing the cantilene from Der Trompeter von Seckingen into the cavernous auditorium with fearful emphasis, while at irregular intervals a humorous someone struck loud banal chords on the piano. There would be no opportunity of speaking with Strawinsky before the rehearsal, I saw, regretting the time I would have to wait in order to get my interview. Then Strawinsky came rapidly onto the stage from the wings, a metallic insect all swathed in hat, spectacles, muffler, overcoat, spats, and walking-stick; and accompanied by three or four secretarial, managerial personages. The man was an electric shock. In a minute business was upon the entire assemblage. There was a sound of peremptory orders; the group on the platform was in its chairs underneath the conductor's stand; a little personage who looked like someone in a Moscow Art Theater performance rushed forward to the composer and started stripping him of his coats and helping him into a pink sweater-vest; Carlos Salzedo appeared at the keyboard of the piano; and Strawinsky, simultaneously resembling a bug, Gustav Mahler and a member of the Russian Ballet, began rehearsing. If he had been late, there was no laggardliness in his mind at all. Never a doubt as to exactly what it was he wanted and the means to arrive at his end! He himself might not be able to play all the instruments assembled before him; still he could tell the musicians how they could get the effects wanted. The bassoonist had some difficulty with the high notes. Strawinsky told him how he could reach them. At the moment when the bass-drum enters, Strawinsky stopped the orchestra. "Deeper," he said in German. The drummer struck again. "No," said Strawinsky, "it must sound the way it does in the circus. You will need a heavier drumstick."

In passages of complicated rhythm, he stopped the orchestra, sang the measure very quietly, and then left the musicians to play it after him. Once there was a dispute. He stuck his nose into the score, read a few bars carefully, then said to the instrumentalist, "You must make it this way" and sang the notes. Most of his talking was done in German, but he spoke French with Salzedo, Russian with one of the men, and indicated the passages by numbers given in very correct English. By the time ten minutes were elapsed I was comfortably enjoying the spectacle and oblivious of delay. The man was abrupt, impatient, energetic, but never ironic either of himself or of his interlocutors; most exemplary in his relations with the players. It was apparent they were working out a little problem together, and Strawinsky had some suggestions which might enable them all to solve it. A kind of interest radiated from him to the musicians, who began entering into the spirit of the animal comedy, and kindling him in return. He commenced singing the words in Russian, even danced a little in his pink sweater up on the conductor's stand. Certainly, at the more startling dramatic entrances, his two feet leaped together off the ground. His arms at all times mimed the rhythmic starts and jerks, till one could actually perceive where his music came from. Renard the Fox, there was no doubt, was himself, grinning from behind his glasses in ferocious joy, and plucking a feather out of the silly vain old cock with every accent of the drunken score.

When the rehearsal was over, I followed Salzedo, (quite as admirable a friend as he is a musician,) and was presented. The little Stanislawsky type was helping on with coats and hat; and I found myself before an oval, olive, excessively sensitive face from out some fine old Chinese print, and a man who sat at once nervous, intelligent, and master of himself. I heard myself saying in French that I had some questions which I wanted to ask him, and that I regretted I spoke French and German equally badly; and was relieved to hear Strawinsky answering quietly that we would converse in the language we both spoke. Several Steinway piano-movers having taken possession of the stage, we retreated with Salzedo to the first rows of the parterre, and across the backs of the chairs I began explaining to him that I had heard he had said he was striving to keep all personal emotion out of his music, that I was puzzled by the expression, and wanted to know more of what he meant.

He measured me a moment, then said suddenly, "We are going to exchange *rôles*. It is I who am going to interview you. I want you to begin by telling me exactly what it is *you* mean by 'personal emotion.'"

I laughed. "But, Mr. Strawinsky, *I* am not a genius."

"Neither am I," he retorted. Then after a moment, "Suppose you went out and narrowly escaped being run over by a trolley-car. Would you have an emotion?"

"I should hope so, Mr. Strawinsky."

"So should I. But if I went out and narrowly escaped being run over by a trolley-car, I would not immediately rush for some music paper and try to make something out of the emotion I had just felt. You understand."

"Yes, of course. But it would cease being personal as soon as one began. However, Mr. Strawinsky, do you impose an intellectual theory of emotion or non-emotion upon yourself when you compose?"

"Intellectual theory," he snorted, as if I had wished to accuse him of cretinism, "certainly not! I don't think I go to work twice in the same fashion. Besides, what is this all about personal emotion? All emotion goes back to the personal equation.

What is emotional for one man is not emotional for another. But there are certain artists who go out before the world and commence crying," and here he raised his arms while a look of disgust passed over his face, " 'Oh, I am such a great man, such a great artist! I have all these wonderful feelings and these wonderful experiences. I see God, the whole and Heaven knows what else.' "

"That's mere impotence." Here he shot a glance at me. "What I am trying to find out, is whether you have any kind of idea that certain things which we call feeling, or the heart, or the soul, are passing out of life? You know, there are certain people who are trying to strike the scientific attitude in living, and working without pity, without sympathy, without desire, even—"

"That's utterly absurd," he interrupted, "the very thing which you are afraid of, and try to repress—that's the very thing which is going to seize you in the end. Anyway, the form of the repression is equivalent to the form of the expression. But of course there is romanticism, and perhaps that is going out of life. But in their very effort to escape from romanticism, people are committing the most grotesque errors. Take Schoenberg for example. Schoenberg is really a romantic at heart

[31]

who would like to get away from romanticism.
He admires Aubrey Beardsley! Just think—he con-
siders Aubrey Beardsley wonderful! It's unbeliev-
able, isn't it? But even the romantic composers
aren't as 'romantic' as people have tried to make
them. Schumann, for instance. I know I could
play Schumann for people so that he wouldn't have
that particular sort of sentimentalism which we
don't admire to-day. But then people would say it
wasn't Schumann."

As he finished the speech, I became aware of another voice, redolent of purest Avenue A, pouring
into my ear, "Say young feller you got to get out
of here if you don't want to get run over," and
found a grand piano guided by several piano-
moving huskies, bearing down on me. By the time
I had climbed over the backs of several seats and
gotten into Strawinsky's row, the train of the conversation had been interrupted. This time I began
by asking him whether he told himself stories or
saw pictures while he composed.

He looked at me a little maliciously and shot
out, "Is this a confession you are demanding of
me?"

"Oh, Mr. Strawinsky, I'm very raw, I see—"

"Well, if it is a confession you are demanding,

here is the answer, No! No! A thousand times, no!"
"But when you compose, is there not something
which guides you? A feeling of form? A sense of
rhythm? Aren't you seeking to draw a line about
something which you feel has an existence prior
to your effort of composition?"

"I see what you mean," he said. "These are questions about which the whole world is thinking.
What interests me most of all is construction. What
gives me pleasure is to see how much of my material I can get into line. I want to see what is coming. I am interested first in the melody, and the
volumes, and the instrumental sounds, and the
rhythm. It is like this. It is like making love to a
woman." Here he glanced about, perceived Mrs.
Salzedo sitting a few rows back, apologized 'humorously for the Gallicism, and then resumed,
"You find yourself, you don't know how, in possession of, say, four bars of music. Well, the real
musician is the one who knows what there is to
be done with these four bars; knows what he can
make out of them. Composition really comes from
the gift of being able to see what your material is
capable of."

"But, suppose, Mr. Strawinsky, I hear one of your
compositions, and certain images of the world, or

of condition, come into my mind. Do you feel that I am reading something into your creations which does not exist there?"

"But my dear sir, who is the interpreter here? It is you. That is for you, and not for me, to say."

"You see, the first time I ever heard the Sacre, I saw machinery and industrial landscapes—"

He interrupted. "Who conducted it the first time you ever heard it?"

"Monteux."

He nodded his head, satisfied. "Monteux does it very well, very well. Monteux has the right idea of the Sacre."

"Then let me ask you one more question, Mr. Strawinsky. Do you think any work, any work of to-day, I mean, which is genuinely living, can fail to interpret to us elements of the daily life, say our relationships with people?"

He sat reflective a moment. "Perhaps not," he said. "I don't know. We don't know what the creative moment is made up of. It may even be anecdotal. You see I myself have not the same feeling against what is purely anecdotal as against what is either picturesque or literary. I feel there is a difference, and I am perfectly willing to acknowl-

[34]

edge that certain bits of the Sacre have an anecdotal interest. But not picturesque. And in the
main, the interest is architectural. That is all.
When people hear my Octuor and especially my
piano concerto, they are sure to talk about 'Back
to Bach.' But that is not what I mean. The material of Bach's day was, let us say, the size of this
hall. The material of our day," and here he lifted
the crook'd head of his cane, "is about the size
of this. But I feel we in our day are working with
our material in the spirit of Bach, the constructive spirit; and I think that what we give, though
perhaps smaller in comparison, is in its concentration and economy an equivalent for the immense
structures of Bach."

Many conversations come to rest with the name
of the cantor of the Thomas School: this one was
one of them. As we went through the door giving on the passageway, and while Salzedo was
talking to Strawinsky about the music of Varèse,
a young fellow who had been listening to the conversation from a little distance rushed up to the
composer, declared he admired his work, and begged
to be allowed to shake his hand. There was a half-
embarrassed moment, Strawinsky bowing like an

oriental potentate, and doubtlessly enjoying, for the thousandth time, the sweetest of all homages, that of young people.

I, however, was still puzzled. Had I missed my good opportunity?

5. "IGOR, TU N'EST QU'UN VILLAIN!"

After having been readily penetrable, Strawinsky's aims had become puzzling. Once he had written music and said nothing. He had been an intuitive musician; ironic, undoubtedly, but moved by and addressed to, sensibility. Now, the world was full of his words, statements, theories, analyses and apologies. The man had grown theoretical, and the music had grown dumb. There was much talk of "pure" musicality, redolent of Picasso's "pure" pictiveness. All artistic problems were to be solved by "pure" means. A composer was to write music, a painter to paint pictures. There was also a deal of ado about the eschewal of "personal emotion"; and some more concerning the correspondences between musical form and the machine, resting on coördination of parts, perfect functionality, and unimpeded watch-movement. The questions put the composer by myself go to show how puzzling when first aired these simple ideas were; now we know they signify the greenness of the grass. What darkened them was, I dare say, not so much my simplicity, as the fact they transformed into conscious aims things unconsciously, intuitively pursued by humanistic artists. Also the fact that the music they appeared to explain was not entirely open to intuition; and not very important. Had it been open, and as worthy as Le Sacre, the Symphonies, Les Noces and L'histoire du soldat, no one, I am sure, saving the professors, would have paid attention to them. Certainly not myself, always aware of Nietzsche's warning that of all Wagnerian exigists, the one least to be regarded was Wagner himself. In any case, they would not have puzzled.

Now, the prime concerns in this case, the Piano Concerto, the Octuor for Wind Instruments, the Piano Sonata and Serenade, and the much "advertised" Œdipus Rex left and continue to leave one fumbling for their bourne and reason. Not merely because of their archaicism. The archaicizing tendency of music in itself is neither good nor bad. It is as old as the score of Die Meistersinger; and although not inevitably bound up with humanism, is frequently its concomitant: witness, its

presence in the relatively humanistic Die Meistersinger, and its absence in the ultra-romantic Tristan. Of late, it has produced excellent results
through certain German moderns, Hindemith and
Schoenberg in particular. Not, however, through
Strawinsky. His adaptations of the forms of Handel, Bach, Pergolesi, Clementi, Bellini, Cimarosa,
Czerny and others, turn one from all "movement
back to" anybody; probably for the reason that the
conceptions are not clear. Some fine music there is
in all these later pieces of his: rigid, strong, pleas-
antly dry and magnificently sonorous music, cast in
Bachian, Handelian eighteenth century forms of
chorale and fugue. All avoid the deadwood of
musical art, descriptiveness, romantic string-vibra-
tion (the concerto is written for piano and brass,
woodwind and percussion, the Octuor for brass
and woodwind); and all have something of the
pure spontaneous movement, the structurality, the
wit and the serenity which satisfy to-day. There is
some feeling, perhaps even "personal emotion" in
the second movement of the concerto, charmingly
modeled on the slow movements of Bach's concerti
and sonatas. The chorale in the Octuor, with its
softly blent brass and wood, is a sustained ætherial
magnificence. Passages of speedy cursive counter-

point appear in the concerto; Jocasta's antique grand air in Œdipus is rich and moving; the instrumental combinations of these late works are robust and interesting, particularly in the concerto, with its puffing, jazzy brass. In the Octuor, the sonorities are not quite as happily balanced, witness the first entrance of the horns and trumpets.

This recent music is not sensual; does not excite the passions. Predominantly reflective, it has been conceived and set down in the best of taste. What is Œdipus Rex other than a triumph of good manner? The brutal, hot, uncouth is excluded from this version of the old, cruel, magnificently worked out tale of helpless blood-guilt. The music is undeluded, unemphatic, architectural. The musician has attempted to solve all his problems musically, striving for externality and thingness. Eschewing pictorialness and descriptivity, Strawinsky's "oratorio" flows agreeably, never hot-colored or grandiose (in the Wagnerian sense), or sensational; bearing evidence of thought and consideration in every bar. No doubt but Strawinsky has found "subtle and probably unprecedented ways of uniting the instruments and the chorus." A most intelligent performance! A lesson in manners; a counsel of humility, sobriety and piety! Only, it doesn't move! It

[39]

is like an illustration, amusing the reflective faculties; not mobilizing the mind, the thinking body. Like all its predecessors, it compels no fresh experience. The region to which all living, rooted works repair in us and which repays the visit with gratitude and loyalty, is never touched by it. We listen, intellectually concerned, delighted sometimes by some felicity of style or form, and irritated by an unslaked thirst. The head alone is involved; and who wants everything done through the head? What is musical in us wants to hear, and is not to be interested by comments, even by Strawinsky's. And if they were merely Strawinsky's! *His* analysis, criticism couched in music, might be tolerable. But who cares for Cocteau's? We want Œdipus, either Sophocles plus or nothing; certainly not the coquetry of a feeble, posturing Parisian.

What has happened; turning Igor Strawinsky into Mr. Modernsky; making one recall Debussy's slapstick *"Igor, tu n'est qu'un villain?"* Was it not actually in the effort to discover this that I went to interview the man, wishing to gain at their source the confidence denied me by the works themselves? I did not suspect my motive, and asked random questions; now however, it is clear to me that there

was an unconscious question and that it was this:
what has happened? Just as well it was not articulate at that time! It would not have been answered. Strawinsky, I believe, would merely have
spoken a little more fully of his new architectural interest, of his anti-nationalism and anti-
orientalism; and not without a certain justice, since
these orientations do lie at the root of his adventures in archaicism. But he would not have revealed
their dynamism, the forces concealed behind their
prim intellectualistic masks; and that was the object of my inquiry. He could not; since their very
power over him, and his own intellectualistic de-
lusion of the "all-power" of thought, flowed just
from an aversion to roots, dynamics: forces in and
without himself. That, indeed, was what had happened: Strawinsky had turned against his own
roots! The psychology of the emigré had developed
in him: the spirit of the man not so much the
physical exile as the exile from his early associations and the past alive in him; indeed from his
own body.—This, curiously enough, came to me
across the pages not of a Strawinsky score, but of a
T. S. Eliot criticism: something about Chapman
or Crashaw, Dryden or Marlowe; I've forgotten
whom. In any case, in recognizing the analogy be-

tween Eliot's bookishness and Strawinsky's cerebralism and archaicism, I saw behind the scene;
assisting at the birth of an hybrid style and defective classicism, neither Russian nor western nor
Strawinsky. In flying from his early associations
and the past alive in him, the emigré becomes mere
head. For purposes of life, this head has to manu-
facture itself a body. It has to make the foreign
its own; willfully identifying itself with that which
makes the foreigner at home in his foreignness.
Since this is early association and the living past, the
emigré is unconsciously moved to identify himself
with the forms assumed by them, sole contact possible to heads. He gradually becomes a fanatic of
manners; called to defend his adopted country's
culture and high tradition; more catholic than the
Pope, more royalist than the king; the intellectual
knowledge, possession, appreciation of that past
becoming subjectively potent symbols of identification. The extreme English nicety of Henry
James, his lamentations over a departed aristocracy,
furnish the perfect instance. Another is to be found
in T. S. Eliot's combination of head-rhythms with
peevish bookishness and a puritanic cult for classic
English expression divorced from a corresponding
interest in the poetic personalities and the human

[42]

adventure. A third alas! is the cerebralism and archaicism of the recent Strawinsky.

A spiritual exile from Russia, forced to take root in western Europe, Strawinsky has perforce sought to assimilate principles of a tradition foreign to him. If others, notably the Germans, are able to archaicize, to go "back to Bach," it is for the reason that the archaic, Northern, Protestant idiom is in their blood, in their early experience; reaching them in living transmission through Wagner and Reger. Not to the Russian; since the stuff of art must long accumulate in the unconscious and lie ripening there, before it becomes fluent and malleable.

Hence, too, the theoretical camouflage: the aprioristic reasoning. Still, even in rootlessness, Strawinsky remains the man of his time. Pressing need of justification through identification with some traditional, established value, is absurdly common. In past years, men sought it through religion. Weighted with a sense of moral guilt, they felt themselves damned, weeping for the sinful will organized in them; and dreamed of bathing themselves clean within a fountain filled with blood. *Nous avons passé tout ça.* Yet substitute for the word salvation the word æstheticism, or structurality, impersonality, classicism, and you will see

[43]

there is no new thing underneath the moon. Instead of ethical guilt there is æsthetic guilt. Men groan with the dark sense of artistic damnation. Emotionalism, sentimentality, sensuality are the unforgivable sins. Men tremble that their works are not acceptable to posterity as forms suspended in a void; tormenting themselves whether grace has elected them one of the hundred and forty-four thousand saints composing the main, the Cezannesque trunk of art, or whether they are predestined mere branches, twigs and leaves? In nightmares knowing themselves romanticists, they feel the whole anguish of the pit. Or, perceiving Aristotle and the old Chinese, Bach, Cezanne and Spinoza in æsthetic glory at the right hand of God, they yearn to wash fatal inferiority away in the faultless essence of the motets of Orlando di Lasso, the *terze rime* of Dante and the frescoes on the Sistine ceiling. American critics run to be spanked by oriental humbugs, and preach to sinners about prose, intellectuality and the mechanics of art. We are indeed a "lost" generation!

The rooted expression *is* justification. Now, Strawinsky had his roots. Renard, Les Noces and the Symphonies were in his own tradition and in the humanistic track. Hence it is not reasonable to suppose that a better adjustment will put him in touch with his own background again. Meanwhile, it is fortunate that even his neo-classical works are not without their contribution, even though it be more a thing of intention than of accomplishment. They are architectural in conception; and the new birth of the architectural interest has considerably deepened and enlarged the field of music. It is a part of the profound, world-wide development of the mind enabling man to think quickly through shapes, lines and rhythms; responsible for the interest of "abstract" art, literature and music. Something therefore is to be learned from Strawinsky's experiments. They are not ungrateful exercises, Moscheles perhaps more than Czerny. Indeed, we have already to thank them for increased capacity to recognize the prevalency of the architectural interest among the ultramodern composers, and to distinguish those most happily responsive to it. The taste we have for Hindemith, for example, is largely due Strawinsky.

6. HINDEMITH

Paul Hindemith's music is the successful delivery of what miscarries in the recent Strawinsky's. To date, this German is the happiest of the contemporaries embodying the architectural and archaic interests. (Perhaps even the humanistic one.) His polytonic concertos for orchestra and for wind instruments, most recent of his important pieces, are conceived as formal relations, and move on contrapuntal harmonic levels to classically dry, precise, snappy rhythms. The spry wraith of Philip Emanuel Bach marshals the harsh, archaically hard, metallic tones of the composition for full orchestra; and the grinding music for brass and woodwind steps off to the stiff beat of an old Prussian military march. And while Hindemith is not a great artist, he is enough of one to make us hold his tendency a sign of the times.

It was their filial restatements of romantic Teutonic conventions that got Hindemith's first hard and benevolent, Brahmsian and Pfitznerish violin sonatas opus 11, and string quartets opus 10 and 16, their enthusiastic, grateful welcome in Germany. He himself was presented to the world as a young Arminius repulsing legions of cosmopolitan musical influences, *Welsch,* semitic, and polytonal. Now, in breasts once comforted by his green pieties, the entirely unsentimental, polytonic, formal and archaicizing processes of his recent maturing works must grate unmercifully. The expansive Germany of the peasant-soul and its appropriate norms, are quite out of them. The new concertos are nonetheless what the unindividual tyro-work were merely taken to be: the new bourgeoning of an old tradition.

Never a poet endowed, say, in Strawinsky's degree with the instinctive capacity for the harmonization of expression and actuality, Hindemith seasonably showed himself responsive to the pace and rhythm of contemporary life. In the crisis of European reconstruction, he produced his first original music; and these atonal pieces, the dances from the puppet-opera Das Nusch-Nuschi op. 20, the chamber music for small orchestra op. 24, No. 1, the chamber music for five wind instruments op. 24, No. 2, and the suite for piano op. 25, "1922," are based upon an idiom directly born of the situation. Deficient, possibly, in distinction, persuasiveness, and the wit that is the better part of economy, Hindemith's deliberately brutal and atonal post-war music is none the less not to be confused with the mass of stuff popular, jazzy, and vulgar only out of an intellectual necessity. Synthesized in an evident striving for order, his mechanical rhythms, drab colors, parodistic accents, jazzy shufflings, jerks, and brayings, interplays of pure sonorities which in their automatic, soulless romance almost burlesque the elder emotional forms, bring the human organism, if only superficially, into relation with its debased, vulgarized, bottomless environment and the bitter time of *lèse-majesté*. Transitional work, of no lasting consequence, these jazzy, savage, second-rate pieces put their tawdry material to imaginative uses. The emotional pitch was sustained; while it was low, it was firm. The structures held together, and the very lyricism the composer could not use, haunted his disillusioned moods.

The character of the libretti selected by Hindemith for his three one-act operas, strengthens the picture of a relentless struggle for contact with actuality. Oskar Kokoschka's expressionistic drama, Mörder, Hoffnung der Frauen, grasps at the root of the after-war sex conflict more grandiosely treated by D. H. Lawrence. Das Nusch-Nuschi, the comedy for Burmese marionettes by Franz Blei, stands in the relation of a satyr play to the vehemently erotic music-dramas of the period before the war; in one place even parodying Tristan und Isolde; and part ironically, part recklessly, wholly accurately, striking the gentle and sleepy tone of contemporary eroticism. Sancta Susanna by August Stramm, the latest member of the dramatic triptych (op. 12, 20, and 21) deals with the obsessional desire frequently coupled with egoistic sanctity, and part of the general breakdown. And like the young Richard Strauss before him, Paul Hindemith has turned to poets with the beat of the times, for lyrics to his songs. As Strauss set verse by John Henry Mackay, Otto Julius Bierbaum, and Richard Dehmel, so Hindemith has used lyrics by Christian Morgenstern, Elsa Lasker-Schüler, and Rainer Maria Rilke.

The jazz age died upon its worshipers. The symbol passed from the attack productive of music of the bitter sort of Hindemith's relentlessly rushing Kammermusik, 1921 with its obsessional beat, vulgar and hysteric gibbering, sullenness of color. While expansivity and exultation were still suspect, shimmies, rags, fox-trots, bostons, as excuses for sarcastic expression and the indulgence of surface-feeling, lost interest for the composers. It became evident that like the universal fascination with machinery, technic and the world of natural forces, the jazz age was merely a stage in the ascension from a life of feeling long dead and rotten, toward a new relation with objective nature and the world-whole. Artists had been "hard" because they were so unsure within. Now, *des Pudel's Kern*, was bare: the new feeling, relatively detached, disabused, serene, and concerned with formal relations. In Hindemith, the expression of this new unity was simultaneous with archaicism. The junction was not at all unnatural. The characteristic rhythms of the early eighteenth century, so spry, robust, and precise, carry the suggestion of a kind of detached, mechanic movement removed from the personal and the grandiose, and still not incompatible with human feeling, with comedy as distinguished from tendency-wit, and with ethical values. The beginnings of freedom beckoned. In any case, Hindemith's adaptation of archaic forms was not arbitrary. They lived in his German blood, and undoubtedly became conscious partly through education and partly through the experience of the archaicizing tendency in Die Meistersinger and the works of Max Reger. Indeed, they had never been entirely obsolete.

Hindemith's new contrapuntal, relentlessly polytonic works eminently supply what patriotic Germany thought to find in his early sonatas and string quartets. His amalgamations of materials received and materials found through contact with actuality, make to continue the high German tradition of a grave, expressive, sturdy music. Once again the robust German speaks. True, there is little harm, romantic lyricism in this temperament. Hindemith is austere, as little voluptuous as Brahms was, and very much less given to expansivity. He is still the "undeluded" sophisticated young modern. No doubt, the complete personality has not yet ripened in him. It is even possible that he has not yet found his style, and that the archaicism is a mere temporary stage in the solution of a psychic conflict. The adaptation of baroque elements may eventually lead him to a fresh style. Meanwhile, he writes too much; and the lack of the will to discriminate among his own productions suggests a tincture of the monumental conceit obtrusive in the good, imperial German male during the mating season and all other times.

But everything of Hindemith's has life and moves. Rhythmic flow was spontaneous even in the early piano pieces with which the Guild ushered him into New York's ken; and in his newest pieces, the concertos for orchestra and for military band, the periods, rhythms and movements sprout as directly from each other as the shoots of the spruce. Often drab in color, his volumes move, amuse, and hold the interest with their alacrity. Of the archaicizing new music, the best has been produced by Germans, Kaminski, the Neo-Bach group and Hindemith; and Hindemith's pieces excel those of the others in geniality, in charm, and in instrumental as well as rhythmic invention. There is a fine roughness of quality in these new uncompromisingly contrapuntal pieces, with their conflicting harmonic planes, and themes harsh, angular and bold as those of Bach's organ fugues. While the architecture does not always suggest important new experiences, it strikes one as genuine and sound; the close of the second movement of the orchestral concerto, the memorable page of the whirring, chattering strings, presenting itself as something never previously given. Above all, the spirit of the music gives one hope. Tender and exalted in the relentlessly polytonal song-cycle Das Marienleben, with its contrapuntal, almost independent voice and piano; groping, dreaming, bewildered in Hindemith's characteristic slow movements; humorous and strongly sympathetic in the Concerto for Wind (that *ave atque vale* to the rough old

Prussian soldier-life) brisk, muscular and alert in the Concerto for Full Orchestra, it assures us that something of the detachment, realism and robustness whose appearance we hailed in Renard and Les Noces is passing into architectural music. And while Hindemith remains still too remote and inhibited a spirit to permit us more than a speculation on the nature of his gift, his music's freedom from personal projections and grandiosity, and humble, dry and every-day character, affirm the presence of that impulse towards the realization of life in its commonest, most universal aspects to be found at the root of all humanism.

7. THE BLOCH CONCERTO GROSSO

Softly thunderous strings and pianoforte uttered a day shod with bronze. They spoke a period of recovered positivity, kneeding the landscape to robust dignity and weight. Solidity and lightness informed the quivering mass within, greeting the extended lines, shapes and growths of the world as friendliest partners. The invisible Kurwenal off-stage chanted firmly "*im echten Land, im Heimatland, auf eig'ner Weid und Wonne, im Schein der*

[53]

alten Sonne!" Feeling of all genuine simple things
was clear across the times: Bach making his dense
gilded music in spiritual vigor; peasants and "little
kids" sporting in the abandon and joy of wholeness. (Toughness and fecundity of earth, that lets
the sharp teeth of her children bite into the real!)
Gleaming snow peaks of Alps hovered near as bellying white clouds. In the pure hay-valley, thick
soles were beating the ground in dance. Cool thin
Swiss beer foamed high in the beakers. The music
seemed to say: yes, the simplest, the homeliest, most
universal material! No spicing! No preciosity! No
sensationalism! Merely, the decision allowing pressure in the biceps, the resolution gritting the jaws!
And serenity floated high over all personal "I,"
prestige and failure. So much alone with earth, her
grief and her graves. So much upon her wide and
corn-sweet bosom. So much apart from her, too, in
regions where life plays; forms move free in their
own air; and, if they will, fugues end *à la chinoise!*
And still, so much with ribald mankind everywhere. *Alors, arrivait un vieux paysan, ivre, qui
chantait comment, autrefois sur la montagne, il
avait baisé une petite fille.*

That was Bloch's Concerto Grosso for strings
and piano *obligato.* In that robust and humanistic

mood lay its meaning. While the piece was not introduced to New York by the International Composers' Guild, it none the less deserves citation in
the present little sketch of world-wide developments made clear by the society; for reason of the
aptness with which it illustrates one of the most important of them. Indeed, it is an excellent sign of
the times, the humanistic, archaistic little work of
a composer of romantic propensities. Sincerity sol-
idifies every bar in it, and still, it has little of the
exotic, barbaric, jewel and drug-heavy qualities of
its big predecessors. Affiliated to a degree with the
Pastorale in Bloch's first string quartet, and its
simple, earthly, unspiced and European color and
tone; a logical development from the formal relations of the Suite and the Violin sonata; the Concerto Grosso is noteworthy among its brothers for
uniformity of coloring, popularity and homeliness
of material, and archaism of form. The work will
continue to be found "Jewish music," without
doubt. What is racial in the Jew must continue to
externalize itself through Bloch as he writes. It will
be equally evident, nevertheless that in no work of
Bloch's has color been as economically applied.
The composer may continue a romanticist to his
grave. Yet in this work, at least, there is manifest

[55]

a Bloch less interested in vehement characteriza-
tions, and more in the common aspects of the
world.

Is this new Bloch desirable? Prime music, his
Concerto most certainly is not. If the piece indeed
is rich weighted simple music muscularly rhythmed
and net of outline, impersonally grave and impersonally breezy; if, indeed, the foursquare little
movements march, thrust from within, it is also
a fact that its emotional line was not born of sharpest sensation, and that no great charge delivered
the form. Bloch's vigor and convulsive stroke
shape every bar, and alternately contract and am-
plify the lightly modernized, eighteenth-century
mold; yet the idiom is never arrestingly fresh. The
counterpoint is amateuristic, too. Many of the ideas,
round as they are and magistrally put to use, appear either slight and undistinguished variations of
certain in Bloch's earlier more Hebraic works; or
of little intrinsic significance. The material of the
Pastorale and Rustic Dances is derived, of course.
The entire scheme is deliberately simple and conservative. Bloch has cho en to abide within long-
established limits of harmony and uses shrill, piercing and "dissonant" effects with extreme reserve.

Yet all one can say for the material itself is that it is generally better in quality than the later Strauss's The chords built of fourths and fifths which close the broad third movement, recall Puccini; like certain otherwheres employed by Bloch.

Preferable to the romantic or not, the humanistic Bloch is present; doubtless in obedience to a compulsion of the *zeitgeist*. And, within its bounds, the Concerto satisfies. Bloch's power and sincerity impose in this piece, too. His capacity for developing and sustaining his ideas is second to no living composer's. Dignity and weight enter what he touches. The new piece seems to show the vehement modern observing others diddling with eighteenth-century forms, fugues and pastorales and archaic turns of style, and then rolling up his sleeve-linen and saying, "Since they insist on humanizing and archaicizing . . ." setting about the business lustily. Each of the little movements: prelude, dirge, pastorale and fugue, is conducted by an impulse flowing unbroken to culmination. A light and iron hand controls the rich mass of string and piano sound, summoning soft thunders of precisely cut sonority. So rich, so golden was the sound that one spied to see whether M. Koussevizky had not concealed a horn in the forest of strings. Here, in the desert of the recent, was earth to stand on, a house to repose in, a loaf to eat. Romantic or humanistic, necessity remains the parent of invention.

8. SCHOENBERG AND VARÈSE

Meanwhile, they played Europe and the New World off against each other at the International Guild. Schoenberg's Serenade began the program; Varèse's Integrales ended it, and the interval was broad as the sea. It was delicate lacework sound against brute shrilling jagged music. It was the latest ghostly flowering of the romantic tradition against a polyphony not of lines, but of metallic cubical volumes. It was, essentially, the thinking introverted solitary against mass-movement in which the individual goes lost; for the reason either piece did its author uncommon justice. Few works of Schoenberg traverse less writing for the eye than this new one, and breathe more thoroughly. The march which leads on the Serenade and then leads it off again may ultimately belong to the company of Schoenberg's paper pieces. But the rest of the little movements, the minuet, the variations, and the setting of Petrarch's sonnet Number 217, the dance scene and the song without words, flow lightly; and bring within their small compass and in the familiar character of the serenade a very personal quality of sound. The mood is serener than it was in' Pierrot Lunaire, and the movement less languorous and less explosive. Nonetheless, the piece's quality is similarly half-painful, half-dreamy; characteristically Schoenbergian; the tone eerie and *sotto-voce;* the structure submitted to intense concentration. The nervous, excited strumming of the mandoline and guitar called for by the score has correspondences throughout the form. And like so much of Schoenberg the Serenade is fundamentally Brahmsian in feeling. The conservatism of the structure, the frequency of rhythmic repetitions, the symmetrical formation of motifs, themes, and entire sections, has been marked by the German æstheticians. Perfectly apparent to the layman is the brooding romanticism of the *melos,* particularly in the Song without Words, and the spook-romanticism of the loose-jointed periods of the minuet and Dance Scene. The characteristic undulant movement, the lyrical upheavals of the line, true, have been compressed by this ultra-modern into minute spaces; stand immeasurably tightened, curtailed, and broken up. But they exist

[59]

in Schoenberg as essentially as in Schumann, Wagner, and Brahms. That is the German, apparently, and the European in touch with a past. Schoenberg is the carrier-on, the continuator of his predecessors' line of advance. Despite the architectural preoccupation distinguishing him from the great mass of his artistic ancestors, from Brahms, even, Schoenberg is the romanticist of to-day; as Strawinsky justly if unkindly denominated him. He is the singer *par excellence* of the individual, the proud, solitary, brooding soul; the lover *par excellence* of the singular, the *raffiné,* the precious in musical expression; of the strange and unwonted in harmony and mood. The sudden entirely unheralded high f, *pianpianissimo,* which squeaks in the singer's voice toward the close of the song Herzgewächse: what is it but a very extreme example of Schoenberg's characteristic processes? To a degree the Serenade approaches the humanistic ideal a little more closely than Pierrot Lunaire and Hergewächse, less descriptive and macabre and perverse as it is. But the divergence is insignificant. Jewelry and feeling of rarity remain; and with those aspects of romanticism, its more permanent attractive ones. Like his masters', Schoenberg is busied in a rigorous search for his own truth, for his own naturalness, and uncompromisingly bends the inherited means of music to parallel his way of feeling. The Serenade is the work of a truthseeker, not satisfied with conventions, and actively developing the suppleness, copiousness and precision of his medium. To be sure, there is a novelty in Schoenberg's approach. His touch is less warm, his emotional frontage narrower than the great romanticists'. He is the man of his hour, and that hour is a difficult and tortured one, less communicable than its forerunners, isolating its members in moody loneliness and semi-mystical adventure. Schoenberg's music sounds as exquisite, shadowy, and remote as Paul Klee's painting looks. Brahms shudders like a ghost. But the ghost has the old gravity and sentiment, and wears Wagnerian plumes, besides.

Passing from the Serenade to Integrales is like passing from the I-ness to the it-ness of things; from a hypersensitive unworldly feeling to a sense of strident material power; and from a traditional expression to one which is independent, and rooted as largely in life as in Berlioz and Strawinsky. Varèse stems from the fat European soil quite as directly as Schoenberg does. The serious approach, the scientific curiosity, of what of the nineteenth century remained on the Continent, is active in

him and his audacious art. Besides Varèse is somewhat of a romanticist. For all his extreme aural
sensitivity to the ordinary phenomena and perception of the prodigious symphony of the city and
port of New York, he has a tendency to seize upon
life in terms of the monstrous and the elemental.
Ameriques, the first of his characteristic *machines,*
resembles brontosaurus, the nasty hungry *Fresser,*
waddling filthy, stinking, and trumpeting through
a mesozoic swamp. Fafner was an elf in comparison.
That is the Berlioz influence: it is significant that
Varèse first appeared before the American public in
the capacity of conductor of the Frenchman's prodigious Requiem. But his romantic aspects are balanced by more humanistic ones. Varèse has derived
his idiom through direct perception, and used it
in interests other than those of descriptivity. He has
never imitated the sounds of the city in his works,
as he is frequently supposed to have done. His music is much more in the nature of penetration. He
will tell you how much the symphony of New York
differs from that of Paris: Paris' being noisier, a
succession of shrill, brittle hissing sounds, New
York's on the contrary, quieter, for the mere reason that it is incessant, enveloping the New Yorker's existence as the rivers the island of Manhat-

tan. He works with those sonorities merely because he has come into relation with American life, and found corresponding rhythms set free within himself. It is probable that at the moments in which Varèse is compelled to give form to his feelings about life, sensations received from the thick current of natural sound in which we dwell, push out from the storehouses of the brain as organic portions of an idea.

His feeling is equally preponderantly unromantic. It is much more a feeling of life massed. There are those who will say, of course, that Integrales is merely cubical music. To a definite degree, Varèse's polyphony is different from the fundamentally linear polyphony of Strawinsky's art. His music is built more vertically, moves more to solid masses of sound, and is very rigorously held in them. Even the climaxes do not break the cubism of form. The most powerful pronouncements merely force sound into the air with sudden violence, like the masses of two impenetrable bodies in collision. The hardness of edge and impersonality of the material itself, the balance of brass, percussion and woodwind, the piercing golden screams, sudden stops and lacunae, extremely rapid crescendi and diminuendi, contribute to the squareness.

The memorable evening of its baptism, Integrales resembled nothing so much as shining cubes of freshest brass and steel set in abrupt pulsing motion. But for us, they were not merely metallic. They were the tremendous masses of American life, crowds, city piles, colossal organizations; suddenly set moving, swinging, throbbing by the poet's dream; and glowing with a clean, daring, audacious and majestic life. Human power exulted anew in them. Majestic skyscraper chords, grandly resisting and moving volumes, ruddy sonorities and mastered ferocious outbursts cried it forth. For the first time in modern music, more fully even than in the first section of Le Sacre, one heard an equivalent Wotan's spearmusic. But this time, it had something to do not with the hegemony of romantic Germany, but with the vast forms of the democratic, communistic New World.

Without the juxtaposition of the Serenade, Integrales would have been a great experience adding to a growing prestige. But that evening the Atlantic rolled. The opposition of the two works precluded such concepts as "Schoenberg's music" and "music by Varèse." One saw two kinds of music, apart as two continents, and based a thousand leagues from each other. Far to the east one saw romanticism rooted in the individualism of western Europe, romanticism that indeed was the gentle old European life. And close, there lay the new humanism, the hard, general spirit, rooted in the massive communal countries: Russia and the United States, itself an integral portion of all one meant saying "the new world" and "America."

9. RUDHYAR

Directly upon this discovery, the irony inherent in things forced itself upon me in the shape of flatly contradictory testimony, borne by pieces by Rudhyar, Ruggles, Cowell; by Ornstein and several other American or Americanized young composers not introduced by the Guild. And I was obliged to recognize that while America fundamentally might be a commune, and as such tend to create an unindividual temper in its poets, humanism was not about to exercise an absolute monarchy. What were Rudhyar, Ruggles, Cowell and the rest but romanticists? The arrant individualism of their work and that of many other contemporary American composers laughing down my fancy of its eventual decay. Humanism might be destined to predominate; might indeed already have the ascendency. None the less it would have to share the throne with its rival and brother. Freshness and vitality were abundant in the romantic house. Its promise too was a decided one. While Varèse and Roger Sessions, and, to some degree, Aaron Copland, were humanistic, it was possible to match a romanticizing composer with each of them. Indeed, the preponderancy of numbers, if not precisely of talents, lay in the individualist group.

Nor was the size of Dane Rudhyar's gift, for instance, to be dismissed; and certainly, a lover of the exalted, the mystical and the remote, more flamboyant and unregenerate than he, was not to be found in the contemporary musical ranks, European as well as American. The great interest of Rudhyar's music lies in its chords. Like that of all romanticists, his musical form is preponderantly homophonic. The accent of romanticism falls on the single perfect moment, which it wishes to eternalize. Proud, solitary, introverted, the typical romanticist tends to see the world less in sequences and oppositions, in linear and contrapuntal forms, than in a sort of simultaneity: whence his greater interest in chords than in the classical related chain. Now, Rudhyar's harmonies are strange, clangorous and metallic: perfect steel jewels of the machine-age. Since Debussy no composer, not even Schoenberg, has piled up richer, stranger, more precious tone-clusters. But it is Scriabine whom Rudhyar most resembles; Scriabine the inheritor both of Wagner's surging, long-distance idiom perpetually drawn by infinity like waves to the moon, and of Chopin's coolly aristocratic piano style. And Rudhyar recovers not only Scriabine's sensitive exquisite idiom, ritualistic elevation and flighted beat. The mantle of the mystic is on him, too, through fascination with pure being and the tendency to seize it in mythological terms. Rudhyar's tumultuous mysterious Moments, for example, show a kind of cosmic emotionalism, an unworldly, rapturous sublimation. Experiences of the great circling cosmical being flash through the achieved little pieces, "what was in the beginning, is now, and ever shall be" seen in the painful, ecstatic, and fleeting moments of birth into the vaster day. In instances, the quick brief minutes take shape in expressions of barbaric power. In others, they come as gropings into darkness, stirrings of blind hunger passive and submiss. Sometimes the quiet tides of the abyss move stilly, the waters be-

fore the spirit brooded over them. Sometimes fires
stream upward with joyous vehemence changing
worlds in their fierce ascent. Occasionally, in a certain number of the Moments, the spark is faint, the
contact vague. These inferior pieces irritate with
the monotonous hysteric aspiration and sick yearning characteristic of much unsuccessful "cosmic
poetry." The failures are exceptional. The great
number of Rudhyar's preludes and poems are filled
sufficiently with the power, wild joy, and movement
of the transcendent state to give it expression and
float us on its tides.

A rebirth, not an imitation! Rudhyar's development of the ecstatic Scriabinesque piano-style is
personal and timely. The better of the Moments,
the unnamed second and third of the first cycle,
and Reaching Out, The Gift of Blood, Zodiacal
Birth, King of Kings, and Moon Ritual of the
second cycle, bring, together with the exaltation,
the opulence and the languor of Scriabine, a distinct architecturality, and a sharpness of attack, a
spareness of effect, and a machine-like thunder unrelated to the aristocratic and delicate expression
from which they spring. Although force, sharpness of utterance and mechanical drive are to be
found in the later Scriabine, it appears in his work

modified by the characteristic spasmodic rhythm. Rudhyar is to be credited with a genuine innovation. Certainly, Ornstein's earlier piano moods, impressions, and dances show similar qualities, mixed as they are with weary racial nostalgia and turgidity of sound. Contemporary orchestral writing fairly bristles with them: Strawinsky and Varèse, and in second line Ruggles, Prokofieff, and most newly, Copland have achieved shining pages with the "hard gemlime cutting of the Greek." The distinction of Rudhyar's musical art lies in the architecturality of his pieces, in the fact that it achieves an equivalent for the clangorous, magnificent pages of modern orchestration in the medium of the piano; and in its earnest of an elevated and objective style. Limited in the range of his ideas and his capacity for extended form, and over-burdened with vague literary and theosophic conceptions, the young composer none the less builds in tone, piling up precise sonorities like mountains; and moving his steely and machine-like clangors with considerable acumen and poetry. His Moments are full of strong, nervous, and perfectly legitimate contrasts and changes of mood, sonority and beat; sudden necessary accelerations and agitations and equally sudden retardations and *cal-*

matos. His full and prodigiously extended chords are without thickness, and as we have noticed, simultaneously rich and steely. There are thunderous effects gotten from a single unsupported voice: No. 2 of the first cycle has fine examples; strong accents that are both precise, and free, rhythmical and bounding; all united with extreme delicacies of the melodic line twisting in mordant-like figures. The tense and penetrating Reaching Out supplies a capital illustration. Staccato and martellato notes abound, producing the characteristic gong-like and metallic sounds. Zodiacal Birth demands piano-roars to be gotten only by striking chords of black keys with the entire forearm, after the manner of Rudhyar's Californian neighbor, Henry Cowell.

We may not, to be sure, too strongly identify Dane Rudhyar and his romantic music with American life. The composer is an American of only ten years' standing, and was bred in France. Still, his work has little relation with that of his Parisian coevals, influenced by the epochal change of sensibility and unsteadied by the general disappointment; marred as it is by the abuse of irony, the satiric and the grotesque, the attempted substitution of surface feelings for feeling, the introduction of facts or personality and transient emotions: and by

a formalism based on a misconception of Bach and
Mozart. Rudhyar's first personal pieces, Ravish-
ments (1918), Dithyrambs (1919) and Surge of
Fire—for orchestra—(1920) possess musical qualities provoking direct feeling. Strikingly Scriabinesque and tinctured by literature though they are,
they lie in the medium in which they were cast,
sustaining themselves in the difficult level on which
the composer conceived them. And only excessive
prudence could prevent us from in part at least ac-
cepting as our own, the works produced by Dave
Rudhyar toward the close of his ten-year domesti-
cation. The machine-like power in them: might
that not well be the response of a sensitive organism to aspects of America? The fusion of
richness and austerity characteristic of Moments:
has it nothing to do with spirit of the America, the
spirit of the southwest chosen by the wanderer?
For me, these qualities are distinctly America; and
it is not beside Ozymandias in the Egyptian sand,
but beside certain primitive things made in the arid
Southwest, that the grandiose clangors and stony
weight of such a piece as King of Kings demand a
place. I find their likeness in the mountainous
American architecture of recent years, and in some
of our paintings: Georgia O'Keeffe's, for example.

[71]

Even the rigid grandiosity of Rudhyar has American analogies: the Plains awoke something of the
sort in the Indians, expressed in the cosmic, picturesque names they gave themselves; and poets of
the cast of Carl Sandburg are moved unconsciously
by vague but similar influences.

Doubtless the testimony of composers concerning themselves and their works is not exquisitely
reliable. None the less, Rudhyar's personal feelings
about the potentialities of American life and the
divinity of the land, freely expressed in his letters,
his talk, his essays and poems, are worth scrutiny
for their corroborative witness. To us, introverted
as it is, slack in spots, full of bad literature and
hysteric soarings, his music none the less appears,
very simply, formed by the spirit of the land. One
feels it springing from the soil of the Pacific seaboard, where they look still further to the West
and feel Brahma near. It springs from the approaching unity, all that makes men dimly feel the
birth of a new god, an American god; not the
old jealous, fighting, egotistic Jehovah and his suffering, expiating, self-sacrificing son; but a spirit
of fire that opens all individual forms, and purifies
and merges all souls together; flushing the hills to
scarlet, bursting the earth with corn, dancing, and

[72]

releasing souls in dancing; the god of old American writers—Whitman with his song of the open road, Melville with his wild laugh writing the tragedy of the god of evil, hate, and retribution; the god of the newcomers, too—warm Sherwood Anderson hearing hallucinating black laughter and the throb of Dionysiac life beneath the stupid crust of the republic; sad T. S. Eliot freighted with a god periodically mysteriously defunct; young E. E. Cummings intoxicated with a pussy-footed god who cannot quite get the step; the number grows with every year.

10. RUGGLES

It is possible to disregard the evidence of Rudhyar's case for the sake of exactitude, and not materially weaken the argument that a romantic spirituality is natural to American culture. The phenomenon Carl Ruggles gives it the firmest of bases. Himself bone of Cape Cod and the toughest of good Yankees, Ruggles builds on Brahms and Schoenberg. Yet not even Frost's poems are more essentially "way down east" in quality than Men and Angels, Men and Mountains, Portals and Ruggles' other solid things. There is a delicacy and niceness in the harmonic element of this music, something neither rich and magnificent, and nonetheless refined, ineluctably associating itself with early American furniture and Hartley's color, Portsmouth doorways and Hawthorne's prose. The melancholy and smothered passion of the eloquently, simply weaving violins in Lilacs, middle section of Men and Mountains, is characteristic of a countryside. So too is the harshness of certain plangent sonorities; and there are instants when Ruggles's acrid trumpets ministerially preach and dogmatize at imaginary congregations. For all his distinct localism, Ruggles nonetheless very definitely belongs to the band of Schoenberg, Rudhyar, Webern and the rest who find the climate of music only at the pitch of ecstasy; and helps continue the great romantic line. At instants strikingly naïve and childlike, as in the Angel section of Men and Angels; at others correspondingly sophisticated and violent, Ruggles's language is warm and exalted, fervent and ecstatic, embodying the characteristic romantic surge and aspiration. There is little of the epic in this work, and much lyricism. And though the individual pieces are self-sufficient objects, it is significant that conception has been accompanied by extra-musical impressions: witness, the quotation from Blake "Great things are done when men and mountains meet" affixed to Men and Mountains; and the lines of Whitman

"What are they of the known
But to ascend and enter the Unknown?"

given the Symphonic Ensemble Portals as its motto.

Ruggles's latest and perhaps roundest composition, Portals, for example, exhibits a sensibility not entirely unrelated to that of the humanizing Strawinsky. Energy and severity characterize the movement of this little string-symphony; both the raucous strident attack and the languid and easy one, are out of it. The aching violin music, thrust out as by some storm of feeling and rising in steep tumultuous waves, never touches one with the hysterical personal disagreeable touch; persists reserved and robust. Still, romanticism of feeling and procedure is dominant and deliberate. Ruggles adores Brahms for his iron melodic line, admires Schoenberg for his subtle rhythmicality; and in his own work proceeds with great warmth of accent and vibrancy of sound. The polyphony of Portals has a tapestry-like richness; the harmonies are singular and mysterious; the movement Tristanesque;

indeed the thrilling sequence of single notes left
to vibrate and die away in the coda have an unforgettable, mystic seductiveness.

Possibly, Ruggles is not to be placed in the first
rank of living composers, prominent as he is among
the men introduced by the Guild. The fault is not
in the romanticism; rathermore in his very modern
habit of theorizing. He will tell you that he never
doubles the same note in his harmony; never re-
peats the same note nor its octave in the melody,
not even in the inner parts, till after the passage
of from seven to nine different notes. It is difficult
to see the benefit of this mathematical preoccupation. The slowness with which Ruggles produces,
and the strained quality sometimes very noticeable
in his scores, is perfectly ascribable to it. Such
mathematical interests are not related to art.—But
while Ruggles is not at present to be placed in the
front rank of living composers, he remains one of
the important native musicians, and his place shines
the brighter after the production of each new work
of his. If his melodic line is merely competent, a
kind of variation of a single figure, his harmonic
substance is of the greatest distinction. His instrumental web is always rich, and most subtle and
sure when he is working with instruments of a

single family: trumpets in Men and Angels, strings in Portals and Men and Mountains. The first few measures of the last give us fluently, tersely and easily what Prokofieff gives all too laboriously in the close of his Scythian Suite: the sensation of a vastly, glittering metallic sheet; "the sensation of looking at mountain sunrises," Ruggles says. Above all, Ruggles's utterances have the conviction born only of sincerity. Unquestionable sincerity stammers, cries, bellows and sings in every blast and every chord penned by him. Through him alone, romanticism would stand legitimated.

II. COWELL

The third of this trio, Henry Cowell, whirler of thunder-sticks and culler of tone-clusters, makes the romantic affirmation from an individual angle. The search for new sounds and methods of composition is part of every romantic movement; and it happens that some felicitations on the discovery of a method cannot be denied Henry Cowell. In an age of technical innovators he cuts a not entirely unrespectable figure. Those tone-clusters of his, sounds produced on the pianoforte with the side of the hand, the fist and the lower arm, extend the scope of the instrument, and offer some new possibilities to composition. Concordances of many close-lying notes have been used by Leo Ornstein since ever he wrote his Dwarf Suite. Percy Grainger calls for tones struck from the strings inside the box of the piano in one of the movements of his nutshell suite. It has none the less been left for the young Californian to demonstrate completely both the qualities of sound to be produced on concert grands by the deliberate application to the keyboard of muscles other than those of the finger tips, and by the application of the fingers to wires themselves. New lovely rolling sounds occur in all of the pieces of Cowell which employ the new method of tone-production: Dynamic Motion, Antinomy, and The Voice of Lir in particular. The Piece for Piano with Strings—plucked piano wires—has a fine dead quality of resonance not to be produced on any harpsichord. It seems probable that writers for the pianoforte will profit by his experiments and enlarge the expressivity of the instrument. Possibly Cowell's forearm method may find itself applied to the music of the past. Passages of Beethoven sonatas may perhaps be treated by it, and brought to effectiveness. Its limits of applicability are nevertheless very strict. Because of the nature of the muscles used in producing the tone-clusters, it is probable that these will lend themselves to effective usage only under the conditions of very moderate *tempi*. The controlling muscles are relatively cumbrous. It is evident that Cowell himself can manage them only under retarded conditions of time.

It is not to be denied that a great many of this young tinkerer's antics are ineffective, and chiefly boring. The thunder-stick performance, for example, was scarcely worth the pains. The religious instrument of the ancient Americans seemed a most uneconomical device. Certainly, its timber was unusually expressive and delicate, resembling that of a wind-machine capable of subtle modulation. As far as one could authoritatively say, it sounded exactly like the voice of God the Father. But so great an effort did the manipulation of the stick exact that one felt Cowell might with greater profit have turned his energies into experimentation with small electric fans, and sought for an equivalent of the soaring sound through regulations of the mechanical devices.

Your true artist is not obsessed with the mechanics of his art, and Cowell is dangerously close to the fatal line dividing the artist from the professor. Fortunately, Cowell is also a bit of a composer, even if, up to the present, the discovery of a method and the invention of new sounds does constitute his chief claim on renown. His musical inventiveness is far behind his technical. Those of his pieces which do not employ the clusters—and To Olive and Marked Passages are the best of these —exhibit a musical helplessness and suffer from monotonous repetitions of small phrases. Those which do employ them when they are not pathetically MacDowellesque run dangerously close to constituting literal transcriptions of nature. Naturalism is the general characteristic of the work of people whose primary interest is the development of a new method of a new instrument. Still, Cowell is not devoid of mildly musical gifts. The people who called for strait-jackets had better be calling for ears, for themselves.

12. SZYMANOWSKI'S CASE

But if romanticism is legitimate; and feelings of rareness and grandeur, cloistral moods, metaphysical and literary leanings, and rapt Tristanesque states of elevation fruitful; why all this pother?

Why all this attempted redefinition of the "musical" position, the "musical" attack, and talk of a new spirit and sensibility, if indeed what "went" in the nineteenth century still "goes" to-day?

The predominance of the humanistic tendency, with its preference for the uniform and regular in style and color, for the grand banalities, subjects, ideas, and emotions related to the general experience of the race; for a more humble, sober and communal approach to life; is undeniable. Major in the early eighteenth century, it was minor in the nineteenth; but some subtle change within musicians has restored it to priority. This revolution alone would attest the birth, or rebirth, of a spirit alien to the predominantly romantic nineteenth century. Besides, it is not solitary in its witness. And while romanticism may be legitimate and true to the times, representative of truthful living and physically practicable, it is all these things only to a degree. Not all the romanticism of Chopin and Wagner, of Liszt and Debussy, is acceptable to us or capable of continuation. Profit attaches only to certain forms and manifestations of it; and least of all to the romanticism of gilt cornices and of red plush cushions "*pleins d'odeurs legères, profondes comme des tombeaux.*" That is incapable of perpetuation. The live ones do not seek to revive it.

The excellent example of its infertility is the violin concerto of Szymanowski, itself not a production of the Guild, yet admirably corroborative of the Guild's revelations. It is almost a success. The concerto is a brilliant, jewel-like thing. You banquet upon high, light, and delicate sonorities rich in effect, upon a refined ecstatic melody, and definite musical ideas and statements that in all their breadth are held from commonness by bold harmonic strokes. The tapping of the singular resources of the violin begun in the three Myths is continued in the Concerto. The composer dandles his solo instrument with affectation and glee, discovering its remote and secret timbers. In the final movement he gives a *contabile* theme entire to the white whistling harmonics. The fantasy and preciosity of sound which he wakens from the old stringed box is spread over the accompanying orchestra. Whatever Szymanowski touches becomes elegant. None the less it is somehow impossible to bestow the fullest consent on what he brings; and the concerto for violin does not vary the rule established by other of his compositions. The music is too ultra-violet, like the orchestral compositions

of Scriabine. There is somewhat of a want of balance between the refined and forceful elements.
The former predominate overmuch. The pitch of
the concerto seems a trifle strained, held up not
without effort in the tenor range. The rougher and
more acrid notes are present: the brisk piping
march-movement which ushers in the work recurs
throughout it; some sharper tones relieve the ubiq-
uitous sweet; yet one yearns for a genuine coun-
ter-weight of harsh good sound. And the ecstatic
Tristanesque lyricism is out of relation. The slow
sensuous mood seems to us insufficiently interwoven
with the fabric of the concerto. The transitions are
either nonexistent or inferior. As a result the ecstasy descends on us without appropriate preparation, without inevitability; and grows less welcome
the more insistent it threatens to become. One
imagines a pair of lovers swooning almost before
they have come together; indeed coming together
because each desires to pass out in burning swoon-
fulness. One feels a too-luxurious too weakly self-
indulgent, silken life behind this easy ecstasy, a
European voluptuousness removed from the earth,
and existing exclusively on the labor of others.
Suddenly it has become bad, hard and vulgar. To a
degree, precious harmonies and jewel-like instru-

mentation are still tolerable in Debussy, Wagner, even in Schoenberg, much as one resents the softness and opulence. There is sufficient muscularity mixed with them in the works of these composers to float them. Something in the spirit of the nineteenth century, some legitimate feeling of material power, some surge of refinement and softening of the passions, may have necessitated this idiom and made it real. To-day the necessity is gone; the pendulum has swung back; the mood has grown harder, less indulgent; mechanical civilization perhaps having brought a greater spareness and control. The whole feeling of sunderance, the ivory tower, the castle and the peak, velvet jackets and green carnations, have disappeared. Every one is living one sort of life; every one is one sort of man. In any case, *recherché*, apart, and precious expressions, and world-denying eroticism, like literal descriptivity, personal projection and all the other deadwood of romanticism and its solitary egos, is not realistic. When pursued, it results only in grand miscarriages. Even Rudhyar, so much the proud introverted ego, is curiously austere and lost to himself in his lyricism; and his rare and strange harmonic substance is free of cloying richness. It is safe to say that whatever makes a musician potent

[84]

to-day sets him on trails entirely different from
Szymanowski's, and in search of other joys.

13. BUHLIG INTEGRATES

Another digression must be permitted. Richard
Buhlig's 1926 piano recital, too, was independent
of the activities of the Guild. But its comprehension of the musical position was so vital, so powerfully directed not only to a reconciliation of the
two dominant tendencies of the day but to an
expression of the single feeling, the world feeling,
underlying them both and embodied in their apparent antithesis, that some record of it belongs
among the records of a society which articulated
those tendencies; worked toward the single feeling
underlying them both; and stands justified by its
findings.

Buhlig's program that evening made a special,
noteworthy balance of romanticists and classicists
reverently, passionately left to their own geniuses.
The c-minor impromptu of Schubert, Beethoven's
sonata op. 110, five of Scriabine's preludes op. 74
and his two etudes op. 65, were set against Bach's
c-minor partita, the last one of the Nenias and the
Roumanian dance by Bartók. A sort of imper-

[85]

sonality, an absence of the personal exhibition, and of the feeling of red-plush cushions and gilt cornices was the bond of union between the two groups. The I was still lyrical, but it sang with the modesty of the less exhibitionistic romanticists: with the warmth of Schubert, almost selfless in the pressive utter giving of his heart; with the loftiness of the last Beethoven so mystically close to the breath of things that his aggressive ego has become almost cosmic; and with the coolness of the later Scriabine, no more the grand and imperious pianistic personage, and feeling most keenly elusive sorrows greater than his own, and the shimmering hallucinations of delight objective as a rainbow or a wing. The places of vantage were occupied by the more stone-like expressions: the partita's definition of a well-nigh impersonal Being, and intimate communication of an almost mechanistically conceived universe through a rhythmic station; the humanism and "objective" position of the dark-toned, earthy dirge and peasant riot of Bartók. The movement of the centrally placed suite of Bach's indeed achieved the living pitch of the extra-personal and fresco-like, and projected one into a region of self-surrender where it was difficult and wonderful to breathe. And while the experiments of the Magyar included a romantic coloration and a rhythmic irregularity and unpredictability far from the feeling of the cantor's time, they too, in all their tentativeness, satisfied through an absoluteness and statue-like externality.

Program and performance were subject and style of a work of art. For a little while, the playing appeared cold. Buhlig was giving no pictures, no interpretations of the compositions he attacked; merely the pieces themselves; and the touch, if passionate, was even, cursive and unemphatic. A sneaking yearning for the opulent, satiny, high-colored and lingering touch and impressionistic pedaling of other performers, particularly of the great romantic hirsute thunderers, momentarily managed to assert itself. Quickly it disappeared. This playing refreshed like running water and breath of hill-winds and sweep of a pure cloudy sky. It was free both of the person of the performer and the willfulness of moments seeking to linger and eternalize themselves. Simplicity brought a greater contentment, the sovereign good of the linked, proportional movement of well-related volumes. The great forms issued in perfectly sensuous definition from the keyboard. One could put hands behind the masses, they were so detached; and the individual tones ran pellucid and exquisitely shaped.

These were the rhythms heard by the composers themselves, the vibrations realized by them in sound; "music" that found a mere equivalent in sonority. So, life beat in them, passed through them, stately or ecstatic, in the moment of union with impersonal forces; and the interpretation seemed no more and no less than a recapture of those forms of union, a transmission of those mysterious trains that surged or leaped or drew through the composers, at the moments powers greater than themselves dilated their finite beings. Contact with fundamental vibrations; yes, that was what was obtaining in the room. With those fundamental in pitch and tempo to our day. For what opened was reality. They were all real: the romanticists with their hearts, the humanists with their architectural lines and shapes and humble universality, the playing of the man with the cool and persuasive touch, like running water. To-day was somewhere between them, taking them all in; and reality somehow in the momentary balance between the two contrasted tendencies of individualism and communism. One went from the recital as from the première of an important creation, in a world whole and harmoniously comprising the streetful of taxicabs, the private bond between two people, the great forces of the world.

14. ARCANES

Arcanes was not performed at a concert of the Guild's, but at one of the Philadelphia Orchestra's. This differentiates it from Varèse's preceding encompassments of the reality of our swift prodigious world through research, experiment and adventure in the medium of tone; Offrandes, Hyperprism, Octandre and Integrales having been first presented by the game little society of which he was the head and motor spirit. Nonetheless the evening Mr. Stokowski led it afforded a crowning demonstration of the work done by the Guild. In merging the experiments of the organization with the general musical stream, and bringing the conservative public the finest, most articulate production of any of the managers of the little semi-private hatchery, the conductor once for all times expressed the impulse and the objective behind that society. The setting was the one usual for the baptism of an epoch-making composition. Gorged with whole live guinea pigs, the sluggish pythons who regularly compose a New York audience, lay in digestive stupor. Only a few scattered hisses and twitches confessed deep slumbers troubled. On the platform, the conductor patiently tugged at his orchestra. Frightened, the band was unable to acquit itself of its normal fullness of sound. (A similar uncertainty had paralyzed it during its first performance of Le Sacre.) Varèse and Stokowski none the less being the stronger, enormous over Carnegie Hall there fell the shadow of—Leonardo da Vinci.

The form of Arcanes is an "immense and liberal" development of the passacaglia form, and an exposition, scherzo, and recapitulation. A basic idea, the banging eleven-note phrase which commences the work *fortissimo,* is subjected to a series of expansions and contractions written for a large orchestra heavily reinforced with percussion. The treatment yielded, in performance, a series of metallic tone-complexes compulsive of extraordinary space-projection. Bristling with overtones as a castle with turrets and a dinosaur with warts, the almost unbearably straining chords shot feeling tall into distances. Part of Varèse's method involved a

[90]

number of air-pockets, suspensions of sound between various thematic metamorphoses; and the resulting volumnear accentuation merely augmented
the excitement of the emotionally conceived relationships between a series of precisely delimited,
dynamically ejaculated sound-bursts. As the high-
tensioned piece proceeded, and feelings found cold
inter-stellar regions, and material volumes signaled
and responded to each other, a fantastic habitua-
tion to the gloomy valleys and arches of the non-
human universe impended. The final variation of
a subsidiary theme, given to contrabass-clarinet,
bassoon, clarinet, and muted trumpets and trom-
bones, came like a long-awaited answer to intuitive
searchings in some unexplored portion of the cosmos; or sudden vision of a new constellation hanging jewel-like before the eye of the telescope. So
largely was the impulse which bore the brusque music of Arcanes that which the Germans call *Be-
mächtigungstrieb;* and so sympathetic it to the
highly sublimated form which the desire to control
and dominate an environment takes among re-
searchers, scientific discoverers, and engineers (Varèse studied engineering, his father's profession)
that it appeared to find the way to its own more abstract and sentimental field through the spirit of

numerical expressions and material symbols, converting them into emblems of larger value.

On the title-page of the score appears a quotation from the Hermetic Philosophy of the "Monarch of Arcana," Paracelsus the Great: "One star exists higher than all the rest. This is the Apocalyptic star. The second star is that of the ascendant. The third is that of the elements and of these there are four: so that six stars are established. Besides these there is still another star, imagination, which begets a new star and a new heaven." As appropriately, Arcanes might have borne the phrase of Leonardo's: "The greater the consciousness, the greater the love." More directly even than from the instinct of control, the composition seems to proceed from the feeling of the unity in the new psyche; and to move toward a form for the entire man of the times. The genuine, large, satisfying, smoky, and metallic sonorities, completely free from the iachism of Debussy and his period; the gorgeous explosive violence, its brutal impulse mixed so considerably with the feeling of thought, of the cerebral processes; the dry nervous vibration of the Chinese blocks; the high erotic tension converted into the impulse to find out, seized the spirit of several research-groups and showed them sin-

gle. Deep within one felt the force which thrusts
up towers of steel and stone to scrape the clouds
seeking here, there, again and again, to break
through the hopelessly dirtied crust of life into
new clear regions. Balked, it returned persistently
to the breach; till finally a new light, a new god,
answered its wild penetrations from afar. That
was the emotional æsthetic man no less than the
scientific technical one, and the communication of
the singleness of the frustrate, battling, finding
feeling evoked a world made one again.

It was at once a revelation of the imminence
of the mentality prefigured by Leonardo, and of
the clarification which a new synthetic intelligence
of the capacity of his would carry with him.
Whether Edgar Varèse is of such caliber, it is too
early to prophesy: and life is not liberal with
Leonardesque men. None the less, Arcanes is music
born of Leonardo's synoptic and comprehensive
type of vision. The orientation in the present universe induced by it is suggestive of the breadth of
his personality. It shows a passion for discovery referred to the technique of art, relating the new
scientific perspectives of the day to the contemporary emotional and auditory experiences with
something of the inevitability with which the

process possessed Varèse's illustrious architype. In
bringing us marvelously close to the bourne of
feeling moving both the contemporary scientific
and the contemporary æsthetic man; and instantaneously exposing the unity of our world, chaotic, divided and specialized much like that of the
Renaissance, his tone-poem adumbrated the art-
work of the future. But so too his society, no less!
It too, pushed toward that bourne; it too encom-
passed something of the reality of our swift prodigious world through research, experiment and adventure in the medium of tone; discovering a frag-
ment of the new heavens in affirming the new day;
revealing much of ourselves to us in finding the secret direction. True, Varèse, the Guild, accomplished the revelation with other's work; while Varèse, the composer, accomplished it with his own.
But the society and the piece had the same young
alchemist for father, and he, consanguineous children.

15. REMEMBERING FLORENCE MILLS

Yet of all the experiences due the Guild, one in
particular stands out, somehow identified with the
essence of many of its concerts, absorbing them in
its own figure. Florence Mills appeared only once

on the serious concert stage, the night the International performed the negro dialect songs written for her by William Grant Still. But the souvenir of the little colored star of heaven gently twinkling, wavering and crooning before the small supporting orchestra, has somehow grown symbolical of what lived amid much groping, thwarted, gesturing activity in the International Composers' Guild, now that life has left both her and it behind.

There she stands, with her fragile pigeon-egg skull, swaying gently, and crooning, warbling, speaking in a voice whose like has not been heard. Larger, stronger, richer, mellower voices have sounded off this platform and off the world's other stages. This one is tiny and delicate. But it has an infinitely relaxed, impersonal, bird-like quality: one knows there has been no other voice exquisite exactly like it. A pure instrument, this; sensuous, but not a human voice at all. In Noah's ark, they said such and such a one sang like a bird, one remembers; remembering that the simile has also been revived from time to time in the course of the world. Still, it is probable that at no time has the application been neater. Here is the very thing, the bird sitting up on a little branch in springtime, caroling; with something of smothered anguish in its tone. One sees two slender legs like lily-stalks, subtly, touchingly intensifying the bird-suggestion with the feeling of fragile, hollow bones. The voice mounts to the head; there, it chirps

"De sun hit smiles f'om high
On de ribber flowin' by;"

and suddenly it is not only the bird, but all untouched nature; cradling itself; relaxed as young animals and children: nature, as it remains in the few blacks and the fewer whites who do not as yet wish to be other than they are, and laugh at what strives to change itself.

So, as she stands there, in our memories, Florence Mills is the Guild. Nature at the moment declared itself through her, for an instant the genius; and that was the Guild, obedient to the promptings of the law felt by artists. She used a common lingo, or, rather, Still used a common lingo for purposes of art through her; and that was the Guild, humanistic in its general tendency, responsive to the present world. She helped establish an independent musician; and that, manifoldly, was the Guild. And, as she stood there, gracious, simple and sumptuous in her twinkling silk blue dress, the old gray man with the scythe leaned toward her.

And that was the Guild. Perhaps the presence of the old man with the scythe really causes the identification. True, it is humanly impossible to regard a Guild, no matter how active a one, with the pathos left in us by the passage of a winsome human spirit. And the International sometimes bored us, and we have hopes that it is making way for the formation of a real American Musical Society, symbol and instrument of the musical creativity we feel developing here. Besides, we can scarcely believe that the International did not have to go. We want to believe that the little singer did not have to die; we want even more to believe musical groups and all groups, the products of powers more under the control of men than those which govern bodily life and death. Varèse and Salzedo have energies left, we say; there are always "others" in musical art; and is not America rich and full of energy? Still, deep in us something knows that these little groups, trivial and ineffectual as at times they are, remain like human bodies the play of elemental forces. They, too, are under the laws of necessity, fated to perish by the force that brings them to a birth. Related to a single station of the world, part of a gigantic, still invisible economy, they give way to a necessity no more without than within them. Hence, something of the mortal pathos, the shadow enveloping the memory of the little singer floats about that of the old saurian of a Guild. It punished many an evening and willing friend. But it was a force. Life moved through it; and to live is to touch others with the antithesis at the heart of the world, with sorrow as well as joy.

EL GRECO'S PORTRAIT OF HIMSELF *

AT a distance, the picture is a ghost shooting to heaven, constrained and projected by two flanking earth-brown masses. Closer, the ghost becomes a high-domed, fine-whiskered head; the brown: fur and velvet of a rich robe; and background. It is the portrait of a man wise at sixty, setting you midmost forces. The movement of the ears unlocks his life to you, letting the world slip with a precipitous gesture of falling shoulders, erecting the seeing head solitary as a lighthouse in the night. He held his quiet and equilibrium against the thrusts of iron where no hand might touch it. All in this body was not gentleness of inclination nor penetration of motives through walls of steel and stone, nor spiritual growth not yet complete in him but mounting to a point. The rose thorns of the flesh were sharp. Forces within the man like those in the world pressed upon his strength, filling

* Recently acquired by the Metropolitan Museum of Art.

[99]

his hours with tension. Driven by a quality of ardent color, the twin pink devils of ears spike the high-domed sallow skull between them, accenting the resistance, counter-pressure, of the long mass they pin. Other shapes continue the sharp motion and shake with the feel of conflict. Pointed forms of livid light, elongated, extended in lozenge-like pyramidal shapes, play against each other. The slender head is built of two pyramids joined at their bases. The nose is a tiny pyramid, broad and sensual at the bottom and tapering upward to a delicate apex. The two pieces of the ruff oppose two small lozenges twisted in convex shape; and each shoulder with its hanging arm constitutes a pyramid. In their sum they compose a dynamic form itself a tall spike, the ghost shooting to heaven, pent in by the vise of ominous background, and unbroken in its upward and counter thrust. We recognize the creator of the strong art of El Greco, the thing of fire and grace and pain, shaken by tension, by anxiety, by excitement, and streaming upward with the ideal aspiration of great Gothic churches.

What this man looked like, how life was to him and felt in him, is the principle of all Greco's pictures; at least that of his major works. The number of his canvases not dynamic forms composed

of many vehemently constricted, passionately motive slender shapes of the sort that made up his
body, is small. And the greatest of them merely
bring the rhythm of the formal autoportrait sym-
phonically complicated and amplified. Two irre-
sistible forces pin in position the nobly, wistfully
consenting Christ in the Gethsemanes in London
and in Boston. Two greenish spikes thrust from
below upon the curving mass of rose embodying
the slender Christ. The immovable rock-like pyramidal mass which surrounds the saviour is in turn
hemmed in by two flanking areas, the one of op-
pressive black spotted with ghastly white which
hold the approaching soldiers, the other of pearl,
fine yellow and light gray, in which the chalice-
bearing angel kneels; the while itself towers upward to completion. And the Christ consents to the
cup, admirably, with godlike self-surrender. He
scarcely needs the outward pressure to make him
embrace death in the interests of life. The painful
rock pointing to heaven is his unconscious will, one
with the infinitely ardent, sensitive red that makes
him love and suffer.—And in the miraculous Pentecost in the Prado, the central form, the Virgin,
is even more passionately borne in upon by the exciting flanking masses of jeweled light and color,

[101]

and given ecstatic upward and outward motion. Here, as in all the paintings of the maturer Greco, everything is excitement, expression, violent pressure and stubborn resistances of color and shape, rapid writhing light, vehement earthward strokes, noblest extensions, spiritual attenuations. The elongations of the flecks, opening, swelling sharply out and tapering again; the rapid modulations of color from deepest black through lustrous red and green, orange and yellow, to sharpest white, then back again from white through lustrous prismatic hue to black, creates ecstatic motion over this and its fellow canvases. There is a continual nervous snapping of radiances on them; sudden flashings and equally sudden extinctions. In picture upon picture the integers seem to reel in disequilibrium, thrusting violently outward in contrary directions, threatening to fall entirely asunder. The rhythm of the glorious Pentecost shoots upward to a corner of the canvas, falling precipitously downward to the lower foreground, to mount again in a series of contractions and expansions toward the tongues of fire and the unearthly yellow apex. The great votive pieces are very conflagrations of racing, twitching, plunging, bursting ruby, topaz and chrysoprase. But their turmoil and disequilibrium is

caught and held in marvelous balance. There is triumphant final equipoise in all of Greco. There is
no weight of violently projected form that is not
counter-weighed. In all the intensity of their war,
the many dancing, struggling, conflicting elements
are single in their effect. One direction obtains: life
moves upward in satisfying, never-ending motion.

And still they resembled him; you would have
exclaimed, "He looks like his pictures!" had you
met him in Toledo coming from visiting a learned
rabbi or Dona Geronima de las Cuebas. Greco in
his maturity was always painting his own figure.
"Narcissistic self-portraits," in the language of
some of our less æsthetic psychoanalysts? Not at
all. Greco sat before nature. Strange, that people
should ever have come to talk about an "elliptical
tendency," a formula for picture-construction in
connection with El Greco, and entirely to over-
look his arch-realism! Even to-day travelers in
Toledo see, riding their donkeys up the granite
lanes and digging the tufa of the surrounding plain
beneath clouds forming "gloomy metallic lakes"
men, women and children with attenuated carven
skulls and long, spare and swollen limbs which
might have been assembled from his canvases. No;
he looked outwards; conceived his work objec-

tively, in the independent terms of a thing. No
painting is more penetratingly corporeal, more
"sexual" even, than his. One moves through tides
of flesh, through tissue, membrane and ligament
before his mighty canvases. Yet no painting is more
divinely pure, abstract, ideal. The limbs, breasts
and flanks are become units of a neutral, universal
medium; shapes, volumes and accidents of a material which, since Greco was a painter and a
visualist, was that of light. Greco actually created
in terms of light. In the very Venetian painting
from which he derived, light never played as superior, as independent a rôle, as that which he as-
signed it. In Titian (see Hugo Kehrer: Die Kunst
des Greco), light is a secondary factor, constrained
to illuminate the chief figures of the composition,
and to subordinate the rest. In Tintoretto, light is
en route toward the condition of form, taking perspective up into itself and suggesting tridimension-
ality. But in Greco, light is form; light is the picture. His shapes are completely penetrated by it.
Light takes them up into itself and reissues them as
conditions of light. The riper, greater Greco
modeled in a rich and tawny, vibrant and solemn
color as others model in clay, running the fluid
immaterial masses through his crook'd fingers and

rigid palms. Are these clouds, one asks, or solid things with all the rooted strength of mountains? Certainly, they are color, pure, independent luminosity. And centuries after Greco, a French painter with an imagination, a feeling for the identity of his medium related for all its peasant-like heaviness to Greco's wirier, more nervous and aristocratic one, say in the Cretan's painting a corroboration of his own conception, made careful copies of certain figures, and was pressed toward the revolutionary, abstract, pure painting we associate with the name Cézanne.

Besides, Greco's art reflects external conditions. The vehemence and excitement are of his time, filled with enthusiasm, religious fervor, anxiety, cruelty and death; simultaneously bestial and delicate; sumptuous in its appointments and bloody in its passions; the period of Catholic counter-reformation and St. Bartholomew with its ferocious soldiers and fanatical inquisitors, and its *percieux* and gracious saints. No; Greco was not examining himself in mirrors. If what he saw resembled himself and came increasingly to do so, he must have found it unselfconsciously, not at all in awareness of how he himself appeared. There were merely—certain objects which tended to re-

lease him, to restore his balance and functionality
(for the reason that they themselves were built on
lines like his own, were balanced and functional in
his fashion) and communicated their virtue to him
through touch. Or, a quality, a principle in nature
or humanity proved magnetic; endlessly fascinating and attracting him, working in on him as he
himself on it, till the relation, the interchange and
osmosis, rendered him psychically, even physically,
like it (marriage has produced such transforma-
tions) and made it increasingly responsive to his
needs and revelatory. We know Greco as the type
of man unconsciously seeking what is germane and
releasing to him and staying by it. There was his
persistence in stony Toledo. We know what ostensibly brought him there. Philip II's passion for
Venetian art suggested a munificent patron. But
the king's heavy gaze preferred Titian's opulencies.
Greco remained. Grandees, churches and convents
occasionally gave him orders. Yet on his death, his
entire property lay in an hundred and fifteen of his
paintings for which there were no purchasers.
None the less, Greco never went again from stony
Toledo and its dramatic skies. He said "a mystery
kept him there which no man must know," and he
was right. He had found his environment, the

place and conditions most fecundating to his genius by their profound kinship with it. Some principle of life responded to its austerity of shape. Before coming to Spain and Toledo, he had been secretly prepared for the harsh soil and sinister skies, the tragic people, the flaming sunlight and moonlight and the fierce temper of life engendered by them. Though he had been well received in Italy and lodged in a cardinal's palace in Rome, the environment at the very pitch of the puritanic counter-reformation could not release him. For his steepness of sense, passionateness and somberness of temperament, and aggressiveness of attitude, Italy even under Spanish dominance, was too easy and voluptuous. That ardor, that seriousness and sternness required a more strenuous and exacting setting. External pressure, relentless conflict of man and his environment, of light and darkness, of life and death, were the conditions favorable to its existence. It required struggle and tragedy and pain, an ideal opponent, a stern challenge, a hopeless fight. And so El Greco sought out the fire where it was hottest and remained stubbornly steadfast amid the flames.

At the cost of life, life grew toward the burning fountain "above." All values enlarged, interior feeling and the significance of things; the one speaking in terms of the other. Greco had arrived in Toledo filled with memories of the paintings of his master Tintoretto, and Michael Angelo. Shortly, a body of broad, deep and accurate relationships between the dark and ardent inner life of the painter, and the alien, tragic, austere and strangely kindred outer world began coming into existence; and his art rapidly individualized from the effect of the growing freedom and poignancy in the use of shapes synthesized from Spanish life. These motives, forms, colorations and movements were ever more daringly and appreciatively selected, and applied in all their Castilian exaggeration, abnormality and elegance; till they began, ever more copiously, to embody the feeling of life on his canvases, and express its pathos and immedicable anguish, inexplicable wonder and grace. Degraded, brutal expressions forced themselves upon El Greco only early in his residency, and in scattered instances. As he grew into middle life they disappeared entirely in the stream of the admirable ones filled with suffering and ecstasy, exquisitely declarative of the unfathomable beauty and pain of the world. His madonnas, saints and saviors are flames; but what is latent in the gentle human heart speaks with matchless intensity in their traits. Perhaps no painter has gotten greater values from the life of hands. Greco made them ends of life indeed; final expressions of the gamut of human existence; their shapes and poses moments of tenderness, weariness, hesitation, tragic consent, saintly serviceableness and devotion, and the cry of intolerable joy. Things and he had released each other, they releasing him into wondrous appreciativeness and eloquence, he finding them their immortal voices.

Perhaps he painted his self-portrait during the time he worked on the darksome king of landscapes, Toledo during a Thunderstorm. Both are works of his old age, and there are other connections between them. The landscape embodies spirit swooping annihilatingly upon the world and making it ghostly. Toledo is the tomb; the invisible in the thunderclouds and lightning more real; death is life; and the present, fading flesh and bleaching bones. What he had to say about himself carries this burden. Perhaps it was something about the forces within himself and in the flesh that drove him to drop the world, lift the seeing head like a lighthouse in the night, and reach up to the burning fountain whence everything comes and returns again? We would like to know. We would also like to know whether as he looked into his mirror and saw an old man, wise, sensual-featured and sympathetic, harassed by the world and still untouched by it, he also saw something which appeared in everything he painted? Or did that immanent idea manifest itself only as he organized his canvas and brushed the masses in? We can not say; and still, what we see in his features and forms as he has represented them, what his marks with their personal reference convey to us, is the identical thing we see on every one of his great heaven-straining votive canvases, where the lines and strokes have no personal reference. He could have quite as truly have called the Toledo, or the Pentecost, or the Agony in the Garden, autoportraits. They equally counterfeited him; while the portrait no less realistically than they, represented the something terrible and wonderful, the form, the feeling in Greco's universe that put the brush into his hand. For, call them what you will, Christ, nature, woman: a form, a feeling and a man remain indivisible and one.

THE PLACE OF GERTRUDE STEIN

GERTRUDE STEIN has not led on the new American
literature. Rather it is the new American literature that has discovered her. The more definite the
orientation of the new men becomes, the more vigorous the relativistic movement grows, the clearer
her figure shows in its seat by the general bourne.
Sport for fifteen years of the journalistic mind,
her vision is patently the common one. Despite the
late hilarity, words are no longer realities for Sherwood Anderson and Wallace Stevens, E. E. Cummings and Waldo Frank, Hart Crane, Alfred
Kreymborg, William Carlos Williams and Marianne
Moore, no more than for the dumb grotesque of
the journalists. Words alas remain for Theodore
Dreiser and the immense body of the public, realities no less positive than they seemed to poor Wood-
row Wilson. But for the great rush of expressive
newcomers familiar with Miss Stein's rhythmic iterations, they are mere signs of relationship, competent to communicate only what lies between the

thinking mind and the objects present to it. The field of poetry has been located in the floating space between the poet and the object brought into relation with him in the quick moment. The reality of literature has been found lying in the state of being produced by the union of the poet and the object of his attention. The function of the word has been recognized merely as that of the definition and relation of something most directly to be communicated by the rhythmic expressive disposition of volumes, accents and effects; by all we term pattern.

Themselves ways of feeling more than intellectual theories, these concepts have quietly helped bring about the cheerful recent phenomenon of a personal democratic American literature not in imitation but in the intention of Walt Whitman. Identification of the work of art as the interaction of poet and thing before him, powerfully invites the individual rhythm of the writer, his way of moving, and profound, inner, subconscious life. It bars all literary formulæ. What is unreflectingly known to the writer in his joyous condition of union with the object is a potentiality established within himself, a pattern of feeling, a suite of involuntary attitudes. Ever singular, the quick moment places all facts in solution and bids the worker reconstruct them in conformity with fresh insight. The consequent effort to body forth his blind rhythmical state very directly produces the poet's individual experience, vocabulary, and response to life, and the expression of the universal principle with which he harmonizes: elements sometimes called freshness of subject and originality of organization.

But these are the concepts and ways of Gertrude Stein! Become clear in us, not the least happy of their effects has been the retrospective discovery of her place in the new literature, the appreciation of her work. Turning literature to pattern and words to relativities, they have shone out sympathetically, clearly in her, visible at the commencements of her career as in its contemporary expressions, and glowing at the base of everything essayed by her during the last quarter century. Her first volume not a whit less than her last exhibits her manful and constant effort to set down with the aid of words the pattern, the motion of volumes, established in her by her subject-matters. If the intuition of the primacy of rhythm or movement among the agents of meaning lies at the base of ultra modern work, Gertrude Stein seems from the first to have

known life keenly, humorously as the succession
of alternate, correlative states. She seems above
all to have *heard* life, recording it as beat; coming
into relationship with it through an auscultation
of objects; and registering what they did to her
quite in the way medical geniuses listen to bodies
to ascertain their individual balances and the coördination of their organs. Character and fate
seem always to have appeared to her finally referable to individuals' ways of breathing and moving: a rhythm embracing the mental, motor and
sexual processes and reactions; larger than all of
them together; fundamentally the counterplay and
interadjustment of basal impulses, the permanent
synchrony of the individual with the universal
forces acting through him. The medium of language, the sounds and shapes of sentences have revealed it to her like people and things. More attentive probably to the way in which things are said
rather than to the pretext of the expression, she
has learned to think through shapes. Words themselves have come to have dynamics for her; abstract
qualities of movement and direction, weight and
lightness, positive and indefinite tendencies. Like
all things under the sun for Gertrude Stein, they

lean either toward featheriness or stoniness; either fly or crawl, explode or sit still.

This American woman's sense of the primacy of rhythm and the consequent conceptions of literature as pattern and language as relativity was probably speeded by the radicalism of the painter Cézanne, electrifying the Parisian air around her in the 1900's with his new æsthetic. In the painting of Cézanne as in that of Miss Stein's personal friends Matisse and Picasso, the artist's problem is seized in terms of design, the rhythmic expressive disposition of volumes, shapes and lines. How strongly the impulse to conceive the literary artist's problem similarly came to her from Matisse and Picasso, is to be seen in her essays on these men published in Camera Work in 1912. In these two pieces Gertrude Stein uncompromisingly set appropriate vocabularies to the task of describing a number of volumes in combinations, dispositions and sequences expressive of her relations to the two subjects, and representative of what they meant to her; and because of the fidelity with which her prose embodied the æsthetic of the new Parisian painters, Steiglitz chose it to accompany reproductions of their art. Yet their intuition must nonetheless have been hers, personally. Her work throughout confesses a strongly individual feeling, the idiosyncratic rhythm which enabled her to understand their efforts to combine movement and poise. While all life is flow for Gertrude Stein, what she nonetheless seems most deeply to feel is unchanginess. Everything breathes for her, but little budges. Everything "has all happened; is all happening; is all happening again." "The only thing that is different from one time to another is what is seen." The flow of which the universe is full is mere equilibration, the steady balancing of the swing. Opposed states succeed each other in a grand drowsiness, regularity, monotony. The ponderous physical forces periodically exalted and depressed return so relentlessly to the point from which they departed that in the whole drugged circling no advance takes place. The Universe stands in slow motion; matter lies mountainous, impersonal, brutal, not to be budged. All the ideas arriving upon Gertrude Stein in the form of qualities of language and relations between human forces have this staticity. Her sentences stand positive, massive, solemn and inert in combination, bricks in a wall and Hebrews in company. They move slowly, at a sluggish pace monotonously reiterated and little varied,

speeded for a beat and then slowed up; commonly
speedless for interminable stretches. When relative
excitement seizes them, as sometimes it does, and
slaps them faster and faster on each other, the
exaltation is low and brief. Promptly the stolid,
tireless march resumes.

The human forces figuring in her narratives are
likewise rigid, massive, slow and set; their movements the passive ones of the pond-lily floating on
the rippling surface of the lake but held in a tight
compass by its root. She is fascinated by absolute
psychic states: individuals to whom nothing happens, to whom nothing can happen, whose existences are the steps of slaves in a treadmill. Most
often we find her absorbed in lives half ludicrous
and half tragical in their staticity and altogether
piffling: existences of women that are a series of im-
pulsive brilliant beginnings and equally sudden
evaporations; existences of daughters spending a
lifetime in freeing themselves from family fixa-
tions; old maid sisters housing drearily together and
circling slowly about each other; servant girls going through the world without heads and the capacity for individual living, and serving, wasting
themselves, perishing like brutes.

Her method of establishing a significant form

has always been her own. While a conception of the novel in terms of pattern was made imminent by the later fiction of Henry James, and while the prose of Charles Péguy is cubistic with the repeated reiterations of emphatic statements, Gertrude Stein's first book, Three Lives is filled with formal relations bearing no resemblance to James', and iterations entirely different from Péguy's rhetorical ones. The life of the protagonist of Melanctha, the roundest and fullest of these three early novelettes, is felt and held directly by the slow, wavering, cumbrous movement of the prose. In it rich sloth and its innumerable recapitulations, the writing well-nigh achieves the effect of a "continuous present" demanded both by the wooliness of mind of the wayward black girl figured by the story, and by the author's feeling about life. Language used in the interests of description is here balanced with language used primarily for the purpose of communicating the direct feeling of things, the rhythmical pattern created in the author by her object. By their sound, their quality, their order and sequence, the words giving external information about Melanctha simultaneously communicate the tragic discordances of impulse in her wandering being. Possibly for the reason that at the time she wrote Three Lives Miss Stein's attack was still inexpert and groping, this first manifestation of her art leaves blurred outlines only in the mind. Yet the grasp of motives and character is already profound, and the prose moves at times with a Beethoven-like density, majesty and spaciousness.

A clarification of technique distinguishes the works composed during the following years, forming a sort of ideal second stage of development. This period is represented by the massive novel The Making of Americans written about 1906 and revised in 1925; by a number of mordant short stories, Ada, Miss Furr and Miss Skeene, A Family of Perhaps Three; by the famous essays on Matisse and Picasso and the less famous ones on Braque and Italians; and by the series of portraits of which those of Mabel Dodge, Constance Fletcher, and Mildred Aldrich are the better known examples. It commences with a mere sharpening and essentialization of the method developed in Three Lives. Particularly in the novel and the stories, Miss Stein seems still to have been aiming at the effect of a "continuous present," and trying to induce it through innumerable recapitulations and new beginnings. Soundings for the mystical roots of character have gone deeper, and the findings have been confided more sheerly to the conduct of the prose. Deep in tone, it manages to give great feeling through anthem-like effects. The former are directly conceived as designs that are both more active, expressive and significant, and more precise, balanced and regular than those of the novelettes.

The informative, symbolical rôle of the word is sharply subordinated to its emotive, plastic one. The word is still used symbolically to describe the progress of the family in the saurian bourgeois epic The Making of Americans. But on the whole the accepted meaning merely permits the author a point of contact with the reader. For their veritable messages the stories and most of the novel rely largely upon their sonata-like suites of rhythms, their slow oppositions of states of being built up voluminously by prose, their slow columinations and the effects of the slight variations in the oft-repeated vocabularies. Occasionally, as in the tale of what went on in the cultivated life of Miss Furr, "cultivating quite a pleasant voice" in a place "where some were cultivating something, voices and other things worth cultivating," the meaning, the truth, is almost independent of the sign-situation. Participles expressing timeless, placeless being come thick. Before the close of this second

period, Miss Stein was dispensing almost entirely
with the symbolical function of language and rely-
ing exclusively on its emotive one. In the portraits
and some of the geographical essays, words are used
almost entirely for their tonal and associational
qualities. If a certain number of words symbolically
related to the subject are included, it is merely for
the purpose of binding together the experience and
creating a contact. It is with a superb logic that
this stage of Gertrude Stein's method focused the
ridicule of the newspaper minds. We never hate our
own habits as much as when we see them in another; and a literature resembling with a grotesque
superficiality her massive sonorous aggregations of
words used for their powerful gestures and clangors
is to be found, every morning, in the seried columns
of the daily prints; differentiated from Miss Stein's
only by the slight circumstance that while she uses
words consciously for their emotivity, her friends,
the journalists, use them for their detonations and
purely sensuous effects under the illusion they are
communicating facts.

There is a third Steinish period, still more daring
and relativistic in technique, dating from a day on
which she read over much long-forgotten early
work, and, as she tells us "did not begin again;

just began." What she had seen must have been a too great knowing of the object in herself; for the latest work seems to be fruit of an endeavor to put down the thing, present to her, in its identity and thingness outside herself, and as a relation of parts. Instead of stressing their mutual likenesses, she found herself striving to grasp her objects in their disparateness. "It is easy to see that in the beginning such a conception as everything being naturally different would be very inarticulate"; she tells us in Composition as Explanation, "and very slowly it began to emerge and take the form of anything, and then naturally if anything that is simply different is simply different, what follows will follow." The inarticulate beginnings of this way of writing are to be found in Tender Buttons, the least interesting and rewarding of her published pieces, unhappily exploited for purposes of sensationalism by some of her foolish friends. A further development took the form of the baffling lists included in Geography and Plays: "In this natural way of creating it then, that it was simply different everything being alike it was simply different, this kept on leading one to lists. Lists naturally for a while and by lists I mean a series. More and more in going back over what was done at this time I find that I naturally kept simply different as an intention." The series seem to have been attempts to set down the rhythm of objects continuously moving from the point of contact by laws of their own. And the most recent of her experiments seem to go toward the spaciousness of form: "And so now one finds oneself interesting oneself in an equilibration, that of course means words as well as things and distribution as well as between themselves between the words and themselves, and the things and themselves, a distribution as distribution." But it is impossible as yet to get an adequate picture of the work done in this "third manner," for the reason that so little of it is accessible. Fragments have appeared, one very magnificent one in The Dial entitled A Long Gay Book; but the bulk of it lies stored about her in her Paris studio, in the spanish chests, and, one suspects, under the overstuffed sofas and behind the Picassos banked on the walls. Yet since there is a single quality in everything of hers already known to us, there is little wisdom in anticipating that the publication of her newest writings will change the importance of her contribution, or assign her a place in literature different from the one she now seems to fill.

It must remain much about where it now is located; close to the source of the new American movement, prophetic of its direction. The more definite the orientation of the new men becomes, and the more vigorous the new movement grows, the more wondrously will it be seen aglow with the vision guiding the movement. Nearer the head of the advancing column, it will scarcely be found. Retrospection will always discover it, not foresight. For, prompt as her orientation in the direction destined to prove the right one for a throng of poets and prosemen was, equipped as she was with a method productive of the most admirable results, and long as her exercise of it has been, Gertrude Stein has not actually solved her marvelous problems. The "expression of the new composition," which, she tells us, "is the thing seen by every one in the living they are doing; they are the composing of the composition that, at the time they are living, is the composition of the time in which they are living"—that, she has not produced to a satisfactory degree. The light that streams from an achievement, from a creative battle fought through—making a situation full of clarity before the coevals and firing their little flambeaux—is not in the monumental pile of Gertrude Stein's writings. Pages and passages of it may occupy exalted rank among specimens of dense American prose. The Making of Americans may secrete the experience of an entire middle-class family's existence. Gertrude Stein's historical position may be assured; as a figure she is admirable, wise, almost heroic, deep. Still, it is not she who has led the new literature into the fruitful new way, or transmitted the spark that set it moving. Nor has she failed of doing so merely because her writings have been slow about finding their ways to the presses. A quantity of them sufficient to insure domination and epoch-making have long been in circulation. Nor have the people who make reputations by receiving creative impulses been unable to ascertain their merits. There was nothing in the situation which would have prevented The Making of Americans from assuming the position open to the epic of bourgeois America among the creative groups, had that spacious and in many aspects extraordinary performance been an artistic success. Gertrude Stein has not been overlooked. Led by Sherwood Anderson, a number of the newcomers have long since made open acknowledgment of the support received from the activities of Gertrude Stein; and tacit admissions of benefit range from Donald Evans who playfully used a phrase from The Portrait of Mabel Dodge as theme of a sonnet, to young John Herrmann, recently arrived with Engagement,* a novel that opens like a page of The Making of Americans and realizes the Steinish ideal of a "continuous present." Much has actually developed through her. The "significant" form of the whole neo-realistic "disillusioned" group about Ernest Hemingway, comprising not only Hemingway and Herrmann, but Nathan Asch, Morley Callaghan, Josephine Herbst and others, proclaims Gertrude Stein an ancestress with every one of its favorite rhythmic iterations of short statements. And not alone the young Americans, but the latest James Joyce, him of the sound-provoked prose, and those of the automatically writing dadas who have not succumbed to "intelligence," the imitation of Diderot or Stendhal, and "le vieux esprit français" owe much of their present orientation and freedom in the use of language to what this dumb grotesque of the journalists first felt, massively held in words, and doggedly pursued all her career. And still, a full creative stimulus has never come from her. Whatever active inflammation the new men owe to others is mostly owed to the painters introduced by 291 Fifth Avenue, and to

* Published in The Second American Caravan.

D. H. Lawrence and James Joyce; even to Pound. To Gertrude Stein they owe much less.

Has she ever very strenuously desired to embody her conceptions and create, herself, "the expression of the modern composition?" Failure to create it has, most certainly, deprived her of an effect corresponding to the profundity of her vision; but has she really craved exerting it? Whatever desire she had, and still has, seems to us to have been always too insufficient to give life to what she has touched. The living flame has passed only intermittently and spasmodically out of herself into her material. Her saurian compositions possess too little of the muscularity, coördination, vibration, the harmony with the laws of a mobile universe transmitted half-consciously from the incandescent body of the true artist to his material, and making it function as a living object. In a sense a majority of her writings are not compositions at all. The component parts are not interwoven and do not form a whole. Frequently the various elements are found arranged side by side. Sometimes they are even partly slackly interwoven; but the oppositions of the juxtaposed parts are so feeble, the interpenetrations so loose and sleepy, that they fail of their objective. At least, they fail for to-day; and it is not to be expected that their subnormality will become normal in, a world ever demanding sharper oppositions, tauter rhythms, increasing swiftness and economicality in its processes. A certain amount of her slowness is justifiable. Having chosen to embody low-tensioned subjects, set, adamantine, heavy bourgeois lives, persons of little desire and flexibility, the whole great mediocrity which owns and replenishes the world, she has had to find their form and express it in the movement of prose; and to a degree she has solved her problem. The tone, the pitch, the quality of language and ideal movement, are precisely, fully struck. Not even Joyce and Flaubert hit them better. Even her unsuccessful works impose by the boldness of their plans, and the keenness of their perceptions of quality. Yet the situation created by these original concepts is somewhat insensitively met. Interest does not stand by the given material, experiencing it and modifying, developing and inventing it in harmony with ever self-renewed capacities for experience. Too frequently one finds the method feelinglessly applied, and is set speculating what the business of writing represents to Miss Stein, an anodyne, a contemptuous belittlement of objective reality, or the expression of a scientific interest:

much of The Making of Americans resembles case-history records. And they, of course, are not exactly spacious.

She will remain the excellent "conversationalist." She will figure as the author of Melanctha; some humorous, delightful stories and portraits; some massive, rolling, monumental bits giving the feeling of space; an epic novel in which unformed material well-nigh obtains without rhythm. But, principally, she will figure as the sort of friend and mirror not herself able to create "the expression of the modern spirit," but, nonetheless, beautifully able to clarify the conceptions of those possessing the ability to create it. As a "conversationalist" her humorous, wise, often profoundly affecting writings have been of great assistance to the present men; and it is devoutly to be wished that the coming generations will find themselves referred to her work with greater fervor than that which sent their predecessors to it. For that which she is supremely able to bring into consciousness, and sharpen, is, ultimately, the great world-feeling found through the Hebrew Bible by Walt Whitman and captured by him for American life. Felt by her in the painting of Cézanne, Van Gogh and their followers, where it dwelt in the shape of an

attempt to embrace the whole world, the life of
the earth as well as the life of the glittering firma-
ment, in the unity of a medium, and to manifest
quivering universal substance in terms of color,
it reawoke in her, the American and the Jewess,
and set her the task of emotionally correlating and
combining the parts of literature in harmony with
it. Out of her writing, as from the tablets of a new
law-giver, there speaks the truth known to Whitman and to Cézanne, to Stieglitz and to the new
painters and poets of America, that the world is
one nature, flesh moving into flesh and becoming
spirit in motion, a great everchanging, ever-
remaining body. It is in her work as indifference
to particular phenomena, and love of flights concerning great spaces. It is there as perpetual search
for the roots of life and location of them in the
great rhythms governing motives. It is in her attempts to seize things in their eternal aspects, and
to hold every little accident in relation to the great
whole of things; to seize character as much as possible as a function of infinity, and relations of characters in terms of great breathing, shifting universal forces. Through its perpetual immanence
there come those bits of expression of a depth and
poignancy scarcely matched by another novelist;

[130]

those renditions of character that in a few poignant sentences give a feeling of the whole of life;
those common phrases taken from ordinary ways
of talk that strike the tone of destinies, planes of
living, whole world-views. Yes, it is to be hoped
that the new America will grow ever more appreciative of Gertrude Stein; since the capacity to
appreciate her performances is indivisible from that
general feeling of spirit, making the American experiment a success.

THE LETTERS OF MADAME MÈRE DU REGENT *

ORNATE, boxed, tall, illustrated, and enriched with
biographical notes, the recent two-volume Appleton selection from the keen, diverting correspondence of Louis XIV's immortal sister-in-law, curiously woke my appetite for reacquaintance with
her through a certain German edition of her letters. This tuppenny Berlin booklet was neither
ornamented, boxed, nor illustrated. One of (inevitably) Die Bücher der Rose, it was printed in
crowded type on poorest war-paper; yet the cor-
respondent recalled by the handsome Appleton
edition was the shadow of the Elizabeth-Charlotte
of Bavaria introduced by it. Was the process of
translation alone responsible for the loss of her, I
wondered, searching out the clumsy little volume
from its shelf? (The English version *read* racily
enough.) A hasty glance assured me I had not been
afield. What deprived the Appleton volumes of the
bouncing, full-blooded presence of the Princess
Palatine, Duchess of Orleans and mother of the

* The Letters of Madame: D. Appleton & Co.

[132]

Regent Philippe, was not the transposition of her
crude, juicy German into the tongue of a relatively pale-faced contemporary England. *That* had
been done pithily enough. Rathermore, it was the
inferior method of composition. The plastic scheme
was the good old orthodox one: introduction; letters like the exhibits on the table at a murder trial;
biographical notes at the end; of the whole planked
down as formlessly and as flatly as dinner in a farmhouse. Of course, no concept was possible here.
None had been at work. . . . Whoever he was,
the editor of the German selection was an artist. He
felt a story if not an organism in his material; and
made the material body it forth. The introductory
matter and the biographical notes, placed by the
Appleton editor in the good old bad old fashion
respectively at the commencement of the first and
the conclusion of the second volume, the German
rendered structural with vital feeling. Inserted into
his text in the form of editorial introductions, critical portraits and running comments, he allowed
this stuff to establish at strategic intervals the historical and social background of France in its Age
of Bronze; describe changed conditions and new
forces brought into play at Versailles; and help innumerable expressions to the point and meaning

[133]

given them by *Madame* (as Elizabeth-Charlotte
was called at court), and by her relatives and other
favorites of her pen. Through this happy combination of editorial information not presented in the
stiff form of prefaces and footnotes, and of the miscellaneous, outrageous, old-world correspondence,
a wealth of reference comparable, for example, to
the prose novel's, was brought to hand. A touching and picturesque, scandalous and humorous con-
tinuity establishes itself for the reader, representative of Madame's life in a kind of work of art—.
We find Louis XIV dreaming that if he but wind a
few of the vines of the electoral houses about his
family tree, he will succeed in placing the crown of
empire on his proudly cascading periwig. We find
the Elector Palatine dreaming that by situating a
daughter in Louis' immediate family, he will have
a spokesman at Versailles and gain the friendship
and indulgence of armèd Gaul for his impoverished
tragic land; consecrated battling-ground of western Europe. We see the prompt if not quite decor-
out conversion of *Lise-Lotte,* his daughter, to Ca-
tholicism; and her departure from Heidelberg for
the purpose of becoming Madame to Monsieur,
frère unique du roi. The story exhibits the triple
disappointment. Louis is disappointed in his im-

perial aspirations: the House of Austria is still strong. The Elector is disappointed in the power of time, reason or the individual to influence the traditions of France; the political no less than the artistic. And Elizabeth-Charlotte discovers the Duc d'Orleans, her husband, in the power of corrupt things in swords and peruques.—The court believes that foxy old Mazarin had Monsieur perverted in youth, to the end of rendering him a submissive brother and subject, and protecting the monarchy from the tempers of another Gaston d'Orleans; thus from another *Fronde*. It also believes that the death of Madame's predecessor, Henrietta Stuart, followed with significant promptness her success in having her husband's companions banished from Paris. And while the King assures his new sister-in-law that Monsieur was in no way privy to the poisoning of his first wife, the assurance has the cast of shrewd counsel to submission. Elizabeth-Charlotte thinks her father ruthless in his sacrifice of her, proving herself something more than a mere princess: but as a princess she makes *bonne mine à mauvais jeu*. For a while the German woman finds some consolation in the kindness of the King. Unique for all time among her countrywomen, she sets a fashion in dress. Then she loses favor, possibly through a pride which occasionally misleads her honesty when Louis burns the Palatinate; probable through the rise to power of the jealous *veuve Scarron*. The great part of her long life Elizabeth-Charlotte is deserted, entirely without credit in the middle of the most pompous, gallant and stylish court in Europe. The impossible husband persecutes her. She sees her only son, the future Regent, married to one of the royal bastards, a fearful humiliation for a daughter of the most snobbish nation in Europe. She has finally to swallow her pride and ask the Maintenon's protection when her husband dies and there is talk of shutting her up in a convent. For upward forty years her private life consists of books, medals, letters. She writes letters daily, voluminous letters, extravagant, wise and scandalous letters. Over three thousand of them have been preserved. . . . Her writing-cabinet is under the roof of St. Cloud. The windows are ten feet above the floor; the walls are covered with counterfeits of the princes of the empire, their relatives and prime ministers; and in the midst of them Madame reads books, examines her collection of medals and writes letters. Sundays she writes to her aunt, the Electress Sophie of Hanover, and to her daughter, the Duchess of Lorraine. Mondays she writes to her stepdaughter, the Queen of Sicily and to the court of Spain. Tuesdays the courier goes to Prussia; Wednesdays to Modena; Thursdays to Hanover again and Fridays again to Lorraine; and on Saturdays Elizabeth-Charlotte makes up the week's arrears. No letter leaves her before she has made a copy with her own hand. Late in her life she boasts to Cardinal Dubois, "When in a single day I have written twenty sheets to the Princess of Wales, ten or twelve to my daughter and twenty to the Queen of Sicily, I am a little tired."

Grotesque, indeed, the evil, pitiful old story with which the editor had given a packet of gossipy miscellaneous old letters a well-nigh novelistic richness, and realized their proud and garrulous authoress for his readers! But turning over the gray leaves of his book, I found that the feeling for life, which made him conceive Madame as a certain being in a certain situation, and given him the grace to let her breathe once again, had provided a further attraction for me. This, was the wholeness of his picture. A humane, many-sided interest in his principal had prompted him to make selections satisfactory to something warmer than a merely scandalous curiosity; representative of several sides of the woman's simple character; and fatal to con-

fidence in the sincerity of an edition which, like
the Appleton, exhibits Madame chiefly in the rôle
of unabashed gossip and scandalmonger, generous
of surprising bedroom information. It would be
gross hypocrisy, to be sure, to deny that Madame
liked a peppery bit of news, that she found the delivery of it less blessed than the receptlon; or that
a good deal of the fun of her letters does indeed lie
in the doubtful matter she blurts forth. She was a
clown; undeniably. She had the perfect Protestant
upbringing; and when, after the birth of her
daughter, her marriage became completely a shell,
her talk became unrestrained. Had she been *gal-
lante,* she might have been decorous, like the Maintenon. Being strict—and no serious charges of
gallantry were laid against her by any of her contemporaries, so sharp in their perceptions and
spiteful in their gossip—Madame let her correspondence bear its singular witness to the virtue it
helped make possible. We in our day can afford to
be indulgent, aware of the probability that her
rich scandalousness was unconsciously compelled by
the mechanism which permits natures desolated like
hers to find a compensation in playing up, and perhaps overplaying, the prevalency of vices. Equally

good seems the probability that it was further mo-
tivated by a half-conscious, cunning intuition that
her tart dishes tasted of more, as they must indeed
have done in those dull times; and were thus certain to beget desired answers and even more ardently desired opportunities for further correspondence. Nonetheless, her coarseness was largely
external, partly the conformation to a time compact of pompous draperies and sheer dirtiness,
festoons and princes giving audiences on their per-
forated chairs; partly a matter of upbringing
(Elizabeth-Charlotte was the niece of Rupert of
the Rhine); and partly the expression of a masculine protest fostered by wedlock with a Monsieur
who was himself so much Madame. You have but
to scan the selections from her correspondence
printed in the German book to be assured of it. It
is true they affirm that Elizabeth-Charlotte doted
upon lard-and-cabbage salad with its evocations of
a blissful childhood in Heidelberg. Her usual nick-
name for Madame de Maintenon signified in a
Rhenish, which Prince Rupert himself could not
have rendered less æsthetic, both the antiquity of
the conscientous favorite's person and of her profession. During zero weather in Versailles, Eliza-

beth-Charlotte habitually took a half dozen spaniels into bed with her to keep herself warm. But early in the series of her letters the booklet brings a number of intimate, touching pieces: those in which Elizabeth-Charlotte recalls to her aunt, the Electress Sophie of Hanover, passages of their common life; in particular those addressed to her favorite half-brother, the Raugraf Carl Ludwig; and these warm homely tones positively attest the writer's humanity.

In a court of neurotics, in a family incapable of seriously entertaining either love or grief, she was indeed the hearty human being; brusque, ironical and proud, no doubt; but inexhaustibly warm, direct, and faithful in feeling. (Strange, the degree to which the position of the enthusiastic man or woman in the present republic of art, resembles hers in Versailles!) It was the Bourbons who were coarse. Beneath the exquisite dignity and decorum of Louis XIV, there was a massive base of insensibility and hardest concentration upon self. It was not so much the state that was the *moi*. It was the royal ego that was the state. And everything emanating from it was established the subject of extremest attention. Never before and never after was a world ordered to mirror more manifoldly

the gestures of a single individual; and his temper
possessed the court and the era touched by him.
Beneath the personal delicacy and intellectual
finesse of Madame de Maintenon there was the
aridity which forever puts her, for all her loftiness, beneath the plane of greatness. Monsieur and
Monseigneur the Dauphin were august monstrosi-
ties; and even Philip V of Spain, most affectionate
member of the family, who during the absences of
his queen fell into melancholy stupors from which
no other woman could rouse him, watched his con-
sort's funeral train disappear along the road, and
then resumed the hunt interrupted by it.

Madame on the contrary, all her life respected
and loved with almost primitive passion the aunt
of Hanover who had educated her, the Elector
Palatine and his morganatic wife, her governess and
her governess' husband, her morganatic half-
brethren, her friends, her son the Regent, and the
two daughters of Monsieur by his first marriage, no
less than her own daughter of Lorraine. Saint-
Simon mischievously pretends that she spent her
hours regarding the counterfeits of the princes
Palatine and other red-faced, bewigged German po-
tentates and their simpering consorts, with which
the walls of her high cabinet at Saint-Cloud were

banked. She fought for her children indifferent to her interest; saved at the cost of her remnants of favor her son from the governorship of the minion d'Effiat, and her daughter from marriage with the bastard du Maine. Her letters entreated the new Elector of the collateral branch in behalf of her disdisinherited half-brothers and sisters, the County Palatines. She labored to advance Leibnitz whom the Hanoverians sent her; and it was with mortification that she discovered that the pre-established harmony did not provide her with influence in his behalf, and that the best of all possible worlds was too poor to afford the philosopher a decent living. Those were not theatrical tears she wept for the basely wasted Palatinate and the poor peasants deceived by manifestoes issued in her name. Nor was it a theatrical denunciation of the wantonness of Louis and Louvois that burst from her in the Dauphin's chamber, when the courtiers came up to torment her with the news of the invasion of her country. Poor creature; but those tears, that denunciation had persuasive power, the ability across the span of more than a century to make Friedrich Theodore Vischer say, "She was moral health," and even the austere Ranke attest, "There was no lie in her!"

Wanting German, is one to forego reading her? Is the Appleton edition then worthless? Returning to it, I concluded negatively. Even an edition bringing merely the candy of the correspondence, as this does: two trayfuls of tart sweets, queer-flavored crystals of existence, piquancies given with astonishing literalness and comedy and irony, has its value. The exhibition of selected aspects, the concentration of special qualities, perhaps figures her too exclusively in the light rôle of entertainer; but that was a part she was vivaciously ready at all times to fill. Here then she is at her most amusing, wonderfully exhilarating, brusque of attack, in grand good humor, full of good horse sense, curious, sound with the inner health maintained amid staleness, theatricalism and cruelty; above all, notably free of any kind of intellectual inhibition. Unconcerned as an unbuttoned infant, she lets every bareness out. *Enfant terrible* of forty and fifty and sixty, she is like to break into her enormities in the midst of the most solemn company. This innocent exhibitionism is doubly our fortune, since withal it is never possible to find Elizabeth-Charlotte of the Rhine anything but a wise, subjectively truthful, realistically minded woman. Together with her seventeenth-century pride of birth (when

[143]

one of her maids-of-honor offered to kiss her hand
as she lay dying, Madame said, "You can kiss me on
the mouth: I am going to a land where there are
no distinctions of rank!") and with her seventeenth-century resignation and stern melancholy,
she possessed almost as a birthright her century's
ease and exactness of expression. Saint-Simon re-
marks it, whose verbal orchestra was enormous beside Madame's fiddle, oboe and drum. Madame was
too full in the manner of her compatriots of *"contes
des feès"* he thought, but freely granted her ac-
curacy of judgment and delineation. Hear Ranke:
"Despite the haste with which they were com-
mitted to paper, many of the letters of Lise-Lotte,
noble in their content, sharp and trenchant in their
expressions, belong among the best which have been
written in the German language." Though critics
may find she imitates James Joyce, who can fail to
chuckle over the letter in which she embodies the
noises of the Electoral chapel singing *In dulce
jubilo?* Even her ignorance was fruitful: did she
not call someone, Cardinal Dubois probably, whom
she hated, "false as the gallows"? Her description
of her son shows how neatly, with means which
Saint-Simon would have called characteristically

Teutonic, she was able to portray a perplexing mixture:

"The sort of thing must have happened to him (the Regent) that we read of in the fairy tale, where the fairies are invited to the baptism of a child. One, wishes that the baby may grow up beautifully; another, that he shall be eloquent; the third, that he shall be learned in all the arts; the fourth, that he shall excel in all manly exercises, such as fencing, riding and dancing; the fifth, wishes him skill in the art of war; the sixth, that he may outdo all his comrades in valor. But the seventh fairy, whom they had forgotten to invite to the baptism, says, 'I cannot take away from this child any of the gifts that my sisters have given him. But I shall so oppose him all his life that the good gifts they have given him will be of no use to him. For instance, I shall make him walk so badly that people will think him lame and hunchbacked. He shall grow a thick black beard and make such hideous faces that he will be an object of ridicule. I shall make him dislike all athletics, and I shall plant evil desires in his heart which will make him lose his taste for all the arts, music, painting and drawing. I shall give him a love of solitude and horror of all good people, etc.' "

Besides, the drollery, the inescapable touch of clownery in the very essence of her manner of apprehension! Was not existence a harmless farce with herself as female comedian? She who was so jealous of her "glorious" rank, and so strict in her conduct, describes in this show-off fashion the laying of the corner-stone of a church:

"I returned last night at ten o'clock from Paris, where I had gone at eleven in the morning to take part in a long and boring ceremony at a convent called l'Abbaye-aux-Bois. It was a matter of laying the first stone of a church which is being built. I was met with drums, fifes and trumpets, and had to go a long way. It quite put me out of countenance. You can't imagine what a large crowd had collected. After Mass, which was accompanied by very fine music, we went to the place where the foundations had been hollowed out. The priests sang psalms and chanted prayers in Latin, of which I understand not a word. I was under a canopy in a place covered with a carpet and I had an armchair. As soon as I was seated, they brought me the stone, on which my name was engraved, and in the middle of which was my medal. Some mortar was

[146]

thrown on it which nearly smothered me, then they placed another stone on top of which I had to bestow my blessing. I confess that the thought of it made me laugh. . . . Afterwards there was a great deal of music and it all finished with a Te Deum. . . . I was so tired that immediately I found myself in a cool room I fell asleep like a dormouse."

Ultimately, Madame's piece of life defies fragmentation much as she herself in her superior-mindedness defied the incompleteness of her existence. It was truly lived; it is too closely interwoven with singular and important historical material not to interest immediately in any form. Possibly in other times life possessed a spectacularity as intense as that given it at Versailles within her own. But certainly in no other did the whole of it go more entirely into grandiose stage-business; and it was Elizabeth-Charlotte's fortune or her fate to observe the author and star of the performance, prime pattern of his age, and his majestic family of hunchbacks, nymphs and sodomites not alone closely, but from the wings. Since she never doubted her perfect parity with all of them, she viewed these historical relatives and their environment without

idealization white or black; and it is this unceremoniousness of her picture of the human comedy
of Marly, Fontainebleau, and Saint-Cloud, which
the French have never forgiven her. How many
accusations of unfriendliness toward France, and
incomprehension of its culture, has it not cost her!
"Elle n'etait jamais Française," says one of their intellectual critics; *"Elle aimait le salade à larde et le
surcroût."* But we who have no national precon-
ceptions about the court of the grand monarch,
find her relentless individuality of great value. Her
prejudices are more easily to be discounted than
Saint-Simon's, being emotional and personal and
uncomplicated by hereditary and social considera-
tions.

Finally, and as permanently as her important historical contacts, it is the strangeness and mustiness
of the individual adventure no selection from her
letters can fail to reveal, which conducts the interest through them. Much in her character makes a
strong demonstration of the immutability of racial modes. A princess, born in Heidelberg Castle,
Elizabeth-Charlotte differs scarcely at all from a
proper German grandmother or coarse and vir-
tuous German cook. One can match characteris-

tics of staunch faithfulness and detestation of *"die
Pfaffen"* out of one's own slender, transatlantic
experience, with those of this person gone into her
Bourbon vault these odd two hundred years. Precisely that, constitutes the appeal. For this
specimen of *"brave Frau"* was enmeshed in circumstances the most special and remote: made party to
a political match of a particularly humiliating
kind; almost deprived of life in the classic scene of
stateliness among golden equipages, processions of
smoking copious dishes, wolf-hunts, theatricals,
balls, and whispered excitement. Even after Louis
succumbed to his gangrene; and her son became
master of the state and she first lady in France,
Madame's existence was anything but triumphant.
A German Stuart, she was invaluable to a government obliged to deal with a King George upon the
British throne. Nonetheless, convinced that women
had too long ruled in France, she rigorously re-
frained from influencing the regent "lest people say
her son was governed by his mother"; and this fine
feeling cost her one of her few satisfactions. While
her son had spent much of his time with her before his government, during it she saw him "perhaps a quarter of an hour every day." Still, it was

not for nothing she was niece to Rupert of the Rhine. She was a *nature*. She had her books, her medals, her mind and her humor. She had her pen. Small wonder a packet of miscellaneous old letters stands the whole gaff of time!

HEMINGWAY'S PERSPECTIVE

Ernest Hemingway continues a kind of prose Goya, jaded, gifted broadcaster of an Age of Hate. Little masterstrokes of exposition, trump-cards of a genial reporter, the stories in Men Without Women parallel and with extraordinary closeness those representative rtiumphs The Horrors of War; through gruesome materials and savage actions upon them, implying a ghastly twin to the draftsman's pain-filled world. Hemingway's favorite situations are significantly of a primitive, martial, pugilistic, riotous and unhappy violence. Like Goya's before him, the imagination of the brute young novelist persistently agonizes with war, battle, torture, the bull ring, mutilation, sudden death and other horrid forms of adventure. Sex concerns it chiefly in its coarse, painful aspects; Hemingway's spirit apparently laying itself at the feet of, and confessing itself inspired by, another common and domineering Duquessa di Alba. If the witchcraft and superstition which intrigued his Spanish prototype do

[151]

not interest Hemingway, prize-fighting, emascula-
tion and drunken riot go far to make up for the
indifference. The barbarous soldiers, the decayed
matadors, the savage peasants and demoniac women
of the drawings recur in the literature. Contemporary in detail, the atmosphere persists that of brute
conflict, rudimentary activity, and the bitter
scramble for sheerest self-preservation.

Dramatic in Hemingway as it is representative
in Goya, the medium involves us immediately in it.
The proseman's phrases are predominantly brute,
stubby, rigid like violently doubled fists. There is
little expression, little richness, inclusivity, rever-
beration, in them: mostly blunt hitting force, as
in pile-drivers. Emphatic, condensed declarative
sentences follow relentlessly one on the other, a
slow steady rain of blows. The vocabulary is rudimentary, largely monosyllabic, mechanical and
concrete, brass-knuckled with raw and pithy expressions synthesized from the lingo of the primitive contemporary types: boys, jockeys, boxers,
huntsmen, policemen, soldiers; and directly related
to primitive impulse and primitive sex. Composed
in Hemingway's excessively dramatic patterns,
chuck-full of decision, and ejaculated as under the
stress of physical activity, they alarm and square

us to the onslaughts of some veiled persistent adversary in the aggressively defensive postures of the gladiator, the boxer, the pikesman. Situations and medium alike make us feel the experiences conveyed by them singularly empty not alone of joy but of animal satisfaction, bitter as sterile sweat, filled with cruciation. The beat of the stubby idiom infrequently speeds up to the rapid, exhilarating, joyous impact of blunt period on blunt period. Neither the forms of the majority of the admirably written stories in Men Without Women, nor that of the novel The Sun Also Rises adequately balance their brutal, dolorous components with quieting, nourishing, fulfilling ones, or move along into spaces signally broader than those in which they started. The contracted norms of expression continue tight and shrunken ordinarily, often with (2) an increasing intensity, (constricting feeling like enduring pain; while the situations add ugliness to ugliness with cold insistence,) and like the two rotten prizefighters in Fifty Grand collapse to a finish. One intuition recurs, triumphantly: the suggestion of the ineluctability of some brute power relentlessly charging down upon the man of to-day, obliging him to a desperate defensive activity with the gloves, the matador's sword, the bayonet, the gunman's "gat," and the reporter's off-hand pen: a kind of passive endurance, a steeling of vital parts against savage thrusts; deprived of rewards other than those of bare survival. The matrix, the enemy, the efficient cause, it insists, has little save hate and pain for its children; urging upon us the vision of a universe "before the god of love was born," barer of kindness, sweetness and bounty than the cindery sullen winter sky of Chicago of warmth; more raw, biting and pitiless to skin and eyes than the north wind off the Lake. There is no joy in it, not even in alcohol, no more than for the miserable rioters of The Sun Also Rises. A cage of forbidding skeleton girders, a menace of steel edges, it damns those obliged to live in its cold, vulgar shadow to ignominy and barrenness; turning innocently contracted wounds fatal, debarring fertile sex-relationships, setting men murderously against each other. Like the passing and coming "champeens" of the prize ring in the story, its successive generations must smite each other deadly blows in parting. Its appetite for cadavers is insatiable. Periodically there must be a dead man; "I must kill my friends in order not to be killed by them," declares the "I" of The Sun Also Rises.

We receive this intelligence no more confidently

than the message broadcast a century since by Goya's art. To both we hearken with a mental shrug, won by the bravura of the account, a little vexed by the shallowness of the burden. It is indisputable that Hemingway's violent world bears a certain superficial kinship to the one in which we dwell as war and a heavy economic pressure continue to shape it; like the one borne by Goya's to the harassed period of Napoleon's campaigns. But we cannot believe in a coin with only one side, or an Inferno uncomplemented by a Paradiso; and neither the Spanish draftsman nor the disgruntled young story-teller present the two faces, the balanced vision. Their form itself exhibits the disequilibrium: sparing us the necessity of discussing final realities, the profundity of the authors' visions or the justifications of the disillusionment. "Relatively genuine in its lack of subjectivity, much of his work is shorthand notes of a talented reporter too lazy to get beyond crude beginnings; and the cruelty shown in his choice of subjects is of a piece with the lassitude of thought rendering the bullfight fascinating to his countrymen": these phrases of Meier-Graefe's bearing on Goya are wonderfully applicable to the razor-edge proseman. The half-amusing, half-disturbing association of ideas of master draftsmanship and of moral prostration, repertorial notes, bullfights, and a relative genuineness, fairly leap from their context and make for the tall figure of the modern. Are not Hemingway's novel and the majority of the tales and sketches in Men Without Women, basically incomplete? Notwithstanding the machine-cut edge and the marvelous verisimilitude (and Hemingway's conversations are realistically rhythmical as those of no other living writer, popular or belletristic); and notwithstanding the many earmarks of volitiency they exhibit, his characteristic writings decidedly lean to one side. Indeed, the narratives pound monotonously along a single track, too frequently wanting contrast, development, cumulation; reiterating experiences till the salt goes out of them. The tedious "Have a drink's" of The Sun Also Rises instance this sort of partiality filling the forms with nonessential motives, speeches and scenes. Hemingway rarely renders the whole of his situations. Almost a small prose masterpiece as it stands, one of the richest of his tales and firm and clean-cut as an athlete's muscles, Big Two-Hearted River goes without some component of reality. It is to be doubted that anyone living in the modern world is able to disconnect from it in mind and body as completely as Hemingway would have us believe his protagonist succeeded in doing, off on a few-days fishing trip. Fishermen will tell you, it is true, that their sport completely absorbs their interest; but the novelist representing such returns to primitivity must necessarily conceive them in contrapuntal form, since the release is relative to an antecedent something; and every point of pleasure involved with a shadowy counter-subject. Hemingway, however, inadequately establishes the ideal foil against which his fishing-trip is thrown.

The case is, that, excessively dramatic in technique, Hemingway is insufficiently dramatic in spirit. His oppositions of character and of principle are frequently weak, embodied in a substance showing dangerously thin. Too many of these oppositions are entrusted to the dialogue, a medium incapable of excessive weight, and effective only when adequately preceded and prepared for by narrative art. Hence many of the stories, "Fifty Grand" in particular, demand a support of the reader disproportionate to the author's performance. But the monumental instance of inadequately opposed and contrasted elements is to be found in the virtuosically written The Sun Also Rises, as powerful in its expositions, as attractive in its stiff-

ened texture, as it is defective in the relationship
of its two chief protagonists, the narrating "I" and
the miserable Lady Brett. All action; all dramatic
conflict; non-analytical; ·sane in its pathos, the
story has all the virtues except genuineness: completeness of presentation. Hemingway would lead
us to believe that "I" has been the victim of an
emasculating shot, and that the Lady, in love with
him, is stimulated to promiscuity by his impotence.
Yet the hero behaves in a way referring us more
to a deep-seated psychic castration than to a superficial, functional one; while the conduct of the
woman makes us infer nymphomania or some other
perversity rather than the mere reaction from a
physically incompetent male. In any case, the material given never permits us to know either character fully; but it is impossible for us not to feel
that the dolorous relation between the pair lies
upon a plane deeper than the material, primitive
one on which Hemingway has sought to situate it;
and that the author's laziness in penetration and
contemptuous unwillingness to account for all his
factors deprives us of at least one half the beauty
of his story.

The convincing Hemingway is largely the earlier
one, author of In Our Time. The later is more

subtle, less obvious in his technique. Nonetheless, the other is possessed by the stronger impulse to completeness. He too gives us a sense of the painfulness of passionate attachments. Yet like E. E. Cummings in Him, he succeeds in setting down the things from which feeling runs in this day; creating a related, balanced picture. Most of the stories in Hemingway's first little collection catch the elements of life in bare, crude but intense opposition. Characters and principles are boxers crouched and proposing fists. Stocky rudimentary passions wrestle for a throw. The sport of the two youths snowshoeing in high Alps is brusquely, casually interrupted by consciousness of pregnancy and the responsibility seeking out the man. A lad sees his sensitive father beset by the active brutality of men and the passive brutality of women. Inside the hotel-room in the rain male and female face each other for a swift passage of their eternal warfare. The sheer unfeeling barbarity of life, and the elementary humor and tenderness lying close upon it, is a favorite theme. The amazing single pages previously assembled in a booklet by the Three Mountains Press in Paris, sandwiched between the longer stories in the Liveright volume and connecting these with the events of an epoch, bring dangerously close in instantaneous pictures of the War, of the bull ring and the police world, the excitement of combat, the cold ferocity of the mob, the insensibility of soldiering, the relief of nerves in alcoholic stupor, the naked, the mean, the comic brute in the human frame. Still, against these principles, set invariably in crude, simple, passionate opposition, the author plays the more civilizing elements. We feel the absorption and fine helpfulness of the handicapped doctor performing a Cæsarean operation with a jack-knife and releasing a child; the tender, subtle feeling for woman's life found among certain of the ordinary people of Europe; the enjoyment of the body in the physical play of life; the seriousness in the young man making him accept responsibility and automatically limit his narcissistic impulse to freedom. And both these forces and the uglier ones are given sharp physiognomies by the dramatic counterpoint; and what certain of them owe Sherwood Anderson is made good by the personal intensification of the intense opposition between them.

There is as little analysis in these early stories as in their successors. The conflicting principles are boldly established without psychologizings. True, even in his first book Hemingway's accepta-

tion of the æsthetic responsibility of getting his
material into action in instances remains near gesturing. His units are not brought into actual opposition in all his pieces. Or, formally introduced,
they remain at inadequate degrees of tension. The
happy relief is furnished by stories like Cat in the
Rain, Indian Camp, and My Old Man. In these,
plastic elements accurately felt are opposed point
against point, and a whole brought into view. Altogether, it is a whole this little first book has to
show. Through a robust dialectic, it makes us feel
together with the blood and the pain the grand
toughness of the earth, able to meet desire, nour-
ish life, and waken in man the power to staunchly
meet the brutalities of existence. Here Hemingway shares his epoch's grim but healthy feeling of a
harsh impersonal power in the universe, permanent,
not to be altered, taking destruction and construction, both, up into itself; and set in motion through
their incessant war. This bald feeling is the condition of an adjustment to life begun in men before
the world conflict, even more intensely necessitated
by its ghastlier train, and natural at all times to the
products of primitive America. Men are reconciled
to struggle through it, learning through it to work
in relation to something in the cosmos, while hold-

[161]

ing themselves tight. The adjustment it facilitates
is not the sole possible one. But it has its validity,
and the rhythms and tempi communicating its
share in its permanency.

(There is inspiration for us in a return, in this
connection, to this early volume. At the moment
of its appearance, it gave promise of an art communicating a feeling of earth and her forces
through primitive modern idiom and epic form.)
Obviously, its technique was derived to a degree.
There was not only something of Sherwood Anderson, of his fine bare effects and values coined from
simplest language, in Hemingway's athletic medium; there was something of Gertrude Stein, too:
(massive volumes, slow power, steady iterations, intuition of the life of headless bodies.) None the less,
the newcomer's prose departed from the kindred
styles as a youngling from forebears. Wanting
much of the warmth of Anderson and the deep
pathos of Gertrude Stein, Hemingway's manner
showed, even in its experimental stage, the outline
of a new, severe beauty equally related to the
power and economy of machinery and the austerity
of the red man. This promise it continues to give,
particularly since at least one story in Men Without
Women, White Elephants, reinforces it with the

exhibition of an Hemingway complete in his material and robust in his form. The fulfillment of this earnest is devoutly to be wished. While assuring Hemingway a place among the hypochondriacs of talent, the persistence of the Goyesque mood might completely debar him from creative effect. The heraldry of an Age of Hate, the paranoiac's world of cold steel, blood and "men without women," essentially remains the rationalization of complete moral prostration, the expression of the deepest psychic languor and love of death. The spirit of brutality is a poor unprofitable substitute for neglected concentration and penetration. And where they are superficial and incompletely declarative of the situation entrusted to them, epic and dramatic form, active beat, and verisimilitude, constitute a miscarriage of the author's business of projection and definition quite as fatal as a onesided subjectivism, wild lyricism and unrelieved analytical procedure; as completely abortive of the reflection of universal law remaining the prime concern of art.

AN AMERICAN SONNETEER: DONALD EVANS

THE veritable elegant is as rare in our letters as the able sonneteer. And Donald Evans the Patagonian released in the quatorzain and in other set and freer forms a personal rhythm, jocundly dashing, reckless, and suave. It walks the Avenue, swinging through all the world, blandest, lightest, proudest of steppers. It is a peacock rhythm, alternately grandiose and nonchalant; sustained awhile in its loud important march, then capriciously, gracefully undercut; and marvelously spirited and exciting to gusto. This exhibition, dandified manner, marmoreal pose, has verve and fire. You may cart away the other dandies, the fat, disgruntled ones. This one, leave; for verve and fire make a music of dandidom.

He was a temperamental member of the Yankee tribe of Thomases in doubt of beauty. "Beauty," to this sport from the Puritanic stem, represented the state of faith known to the artists: release into life vaster than the personal; apprehension of changeless law through the individual adventure. "Could I enlist a Battalion of Irreproachables," he let the introduction to the wartime edition of his Sonnets from the Patagonian say, "whose uniform should be walking suit, top hat and pumps, and their only weapon an ebony stick, and sail to-morrow, we should march down Unter den Linden in a month, provided wrapped in our kerchiefs we carried the Gospel of Beauty, and a nonchalance in the knot of our cravats." That was his humorously affected fashion of affirming the miraculous power of the religious sense, the deep immutable imper-sonality toward which he groped and which eluded him in life. The makings existed in him. The rhythm of the Patagonian sonnets streams into the world at a brilliant elevation. Yet the feelings would not issue warmly. Perhaps we have to do with one of the unfortunate sensuous devils per-petually in trouble with themselves; aware of hav-ing sacrificed to perishable emotions; familiar from the cradle with a sense of guilt and of damnation; prisoners to vanity's last and firmest shackles, the conviction of having failed of achieving what others had a right to expect and was owing themselves. Evans' beginning to an autoportrait runs:

⌈165⌉

"Wistfully shimmering, shamelessly wise and weak,
He lives in pawn, pledging a battered name;
He loves his failures as one might love fame . . ."

In this condition of torment, conscious of serene regions and incapable of attaining them, sensitive feelings could not have the strength flowing from the conviction which comes from universality. Release was to be found only in the quasi-decorative use of the talents, in agreeable self-exhibition, in the dashing and nonchalant air of the fabled Bond Street walker absolved of all reproach through the faultless conduct of a "clouded" cane. Hence, the form of his poetry, the Patagonianism, the air of elegant hard-boiling, the reckless fondling of the superior grotesques of modern life: Igor Vyvian, the heuetontimoroumenos; the brilliant lady destructive in her hysterical self-indulgence and tragic mountainous mole-hills; and the gentleman who "polished snubs till they were regnant art." The machinery gave his impulses a unity. The flaunt of impassivity permitted him to visit the weak scenes of his life in complete superiority; to portray the compromitments of clever men, and the dangerous tricks of feminine *amour-propre* which made it up; and to give out his riches and "dance along the boulevard" over the pain he could not quell.

> "Masters are makeshifts and a path to tread
> For blue pumps that are ardent for the air.
> Features are fixtures when the face is fled,
> And we are left the husks of tarnished hair.
> But he is one who lusts uncomforted
> To kiss the naked phrase quite unaware."

It is a comedy he proposes, charming precisely for the reason he wished to mislead none by his masquerade. The great fun of the Patagonian sonnets flows from the excruciating solemnity with which he advertises his emotions the frivolous attitudes of an "incurable *poseur*," letting

> "His calm moustache point to the ironies
> And a fawn-coloured laugh suck in the night
> Full of the riant mists that turn to white
> In brief lost battles with banalities."

Observe how slyly he overplays the rare, exaggerated coxcomb, 1890 metaphor, adjective or noun:

> "Forgetting her mauve vows the Fania fled
> Taking away her moonlight scarves with her—

[167]

There was no joy left in the calendar
And life was but an orchid which was dead.
Even our pious peacocks went unfed. . . ."

An impeccable art? A most uneven one, particularly in the sonnets. Choppy lines, tending to halt with the rhyme, stand among suavely flowing ones. Rhymes too facile, recalling the indissoluble union of strife with life, clash with distinguished correspondences of sound. Images and terms, too, florid beyond the experience of even an ironic cavalier, detract from the surprise of images born of sensation:

"The flutes were hushed that mimed the orange moon"

or

"Chastely he spends an hour every day
Erecting tombstones to carnalities."

Only the tenderness and quiet music of the birthday piece commencing:

"There is what is, and what there is is fair,"

wins pardon for the unacknowledged debt to Gertrude Stein and The Portrait of Mabel Dodge. The diablerie wipes all remonstrance out. Some of the sonnets are fanfares defiant in the curve of trumpeted emotion. Or brigantines full-sailed and aflutter with all the pennants of pride. The very lines of songs of ruth tilt upward:

"Time that had marked him for the least of sages
　Pointed the hour . . ."

Ultimate verses stand acrobats at the close of vaudeville turns, "*Voilà!*" upon their lips, twisted wrists and fingers pointed starward:

"And then I danced along the boulevard!"

and

"She triumphed in the tragic turnip field!"

and

"He felt he had used the finest snub of all!"

The *élan,* mock-heroic in instances, in others approaches lyricism:

"Crapulous hands reach out to strangle thee,
　And every moment is a winding sheet
　With bats to chant corruption's litany.
　Be thou a torch to flash fanfaronade;
　And as the earth crumbles beneath thy feet
　Flaunt thou the glitter of a new brocade!"

Burlesque, mock-heroic, or direct and lyrical, the
feeling of life moves recklessly, swaggeringly
"across the rotting pads in the lily lake."

Kreymborg has remarked the precision and
beautiful modeling of Evans' phrases. His senses
must have been aware of magnificent textures,
billowing grain, voices "fleet-limbed and immacu-
late," loveliness of pearls "sheer and shimmering."
The words come suave as silk: "Song for the min-
now and a crystal pool," "Repeated payment of
inutile toll," "haunting coins to meagre beauty
flung," Evans' style had the sensuous, textural quality born of relativistic practice. While his first
poems have the wan, unhealthy complexion of the
verse of the Symons period, they do reveal the first
indications of a daring in the use of words for their
color, sound and texture; and in his later pieces,
perhaps under the influence of his friend Allan Nor-
ton's Saloon Sonnets; certainly under the influence
of that notable modern pioneer-woman Gertrude
Stein, the emotional usage of the word, its function as the expression of what exists in the poet at
the moment of his union with the object, is fairly
advanced. As extreme a practitioner of verbal rel-
ativism as either Gertrude Stein, or as his fellow-

[170]

poets Ezra Pound, Wallace Stevens and Edith Sit-
well, Evans never became. But he was one of the
first of contemporaries to find himself through the
new way of expression destined to liberate not only
himself and some few others, but to create a new
poetic art. He used the detonations of words in his
own intention, recording his own rich, precious,
mordant little note. And while the timbres, the
substances, the verbal orchestration of Stevens,
Hart Crane, and E. E. Cummings leaves Evans behind in the race of textural modern poetry, he stays
in it with defiant colors.

It is as a dandy, then; perhaps a unique example,
that he figures in American literature. True, his
last little collection, Two Deaths in the Bronx,
introduces, in one single satisfying expression, a
new aspect of Donald Evans. The poet of Two
Deaths is master of him of the Sonnets in several
faculties. He indulges more infrequently in emotional rhetoric, is obliged to find fewer stop-gap
phrases. If there is greater poison and pain in his
ideas, there is greater polish and effortlessness of
handling. Irritations scream beneath an ivory surface. Over the hell of emotional impotence, waxed
mustache-tips approach a perfect point. And in

the shade of ironism a simpler flower grows. The amazing new note, the truly major note come at length to Evans, is found at its roundest in the first of the two poems For the Haunting of Mauna, beginning

> "Suave body of the Queen, she gave me you,
>   Misting in still warm rains of tenderness,
>   But kept herself, and we are each betrayed."

Here for the first time passion is shot with warmth. There had been sensuous feeling, but never an apprehension of beauty as selfless and pierced with the pangs of tenderness and impermanency. Had Evans managed to survive another decade, he might have advanced broadly upon the positive high road reached at last. Yet, in the words of a modern chronicle, "not many days later, Donald was found dead in his room—and rumor reported that his own hand had concerned itself with the end." But if it is in the figure of the "fawn-colored laugh sucking in the night" he must remain, it is to no disadvantage, and with a fine distinction. "The ablest of our sonneteers," Kreymborg has dubbed him; praising his quatorzains, "the form no American has ever surpassed him in." For us, if an American

Suckling exists, it is Donald Evans, with his flare.
What matter what he *said?* The verve, suavity,
reckless music return upon him permanently to
clothe him.

THE CITY: WITH A GLANCE AT
HONEGGER

OAKS were standing in kingly flame over the fields as I left. The cityward trip for the purpose of attending the first Sunday afternoon concert of the League of Composers, and the first perform- ance of Le Roi David by Honegger, was unattrac- tive; seven hours of travel had never before seemed so forbidding; and I supposed that it was the fiery copper of the regal trees that was making me balk. The tower of steep stone buildings above the ar- rival platform in Grand Central gave my rational- ization the first lie. The lands in very brown Octo- ber, had a puissant rival. There had never been a place like this New York: Flaubert's Carthage all of high sacrificial altars; and I saw that no mere attachment to scenery had opposed the trip. The Sunday sight of the auction room in Anderson Galleries, prepared for the little concert, gave it the second lie. I remembered that whatever the music, you invariably see all of your friends all together

all in one room at the concerts of the League of
Composers, and that is always ravishing. In a
world where things relentlessly flow, it is a rare
privilege to know so much standing relatively un-
changed: theories, facial expressions, maladjust-
ments and self-satisfactions; and again this afternoon some of the music proved itself worthy of
attention. Settings of Czech and Hungarian folksongs retained the freshness and essentiality of the
expressions selected by the experience of many
lives. *"Das Echte bleibt der Nachwelt unverloren!"*
There was a new sonata for violin and piano by
an American lady which showed progress, all the
more marvelously since it was impossible to feel
that the gentle composer would ever arrive any-
where at all. There were some Jazz Berries (bold
titular contemporaneousness!) by an American pupil of Busoni's; impressive as contraptions, and as
the products of will, perhaps of unwill. The middle
section of the string quartet by a new young
Italian seemed looking for use in a veristic opera
as atmosphere for a night in Naples when there
was absolutely "nothing doing," and a single taper
burned stilly before the Madonna's shrine. The
piece de resistance, a piano sonata by the leading
European composer of the hour, likewise made lis-

tening agreeable. A bit of sophisticated Piccinism,
it recalled Bach fantasias and the Schumann toc-
cata with much archness of the rococo. . . . None
the less throughout the little concert and among
good friends, ribaldry clutched my bowels. Though
it obviously had not been the heraldic trees and
the richly pelted hills that had disaffected me from
the market place of New York; though my pretext for throwing up the trip was revealed the
poorest one; sense was present somewhere in my
unwillingness, I saw; shaking with suppressed mirth
and thinking I had discovered the true ground in
an intuition of the conventionality of most of the
music. It was unquestionably written on formulas,
the composers patterning their expressions on those
of the revolutionists of ten years since established
as an academy. First theme, a little rushing, tinkling Petrushka; popular and *degagée*. Second,
lyric theme, some Chinese-laundry music, penta-
tonic and gastritic; and the three other movements
come easily. Even the sonata of the great modern
Piccinist, like so much of his new classicizing work,
was music dehydrated through the mechanical
imposition of forms intellectually conceived and
adopted. Everywhere, a great want of sensibility.
No necessity, hence no thematic invention. No

[176]

relation of the inner realm to the world, with its gift of style. The street outside with its herds of taxis and limousines, its traffic-signals, demolition and riveting, was it not able to give more of an æsthetic experience at any hour of the day? And my soul reared, and on its hind legs, bellowed, "Does it have to be composed?" as I went out of the door.

A few hours it was pat that the artists with their formalism were responsible for the detestability of the market of New York. But a fact more basic was working for recognition; suddenly my attention moved from the artists to more massive bodies. It was at the Bellows Memorial Show at the Museum, taken in during the hours before Le Roi David. In a vast gallery the crass name of the brushman was belched by an array of paintings of which perhaps three bore an uncertain faint relation to art. All of them made flashy appeals through sentimental subjects; in each a male coquetted with an ostentation of muscularity, tough talk, he-manliness. The great *blaa* of the exhibition came heavy with the downbearing might of a corporation; and in defending myself against the prestige of a collection of old masters created by other men and times, now being used to establish work embodying no ideas, I recognized the institutional share in the heady toxin of New York. If the artists were misusing an instrument capable of the grandest communications of life, with how much more deadly an effect were the old rascals supposed to guard the Muses—museum directors, teachers and organs of publicity and renown, dissipating the feeling of life by their loud insistence not only on certain individuals, but invariably the wrong individuals: the ones least able, least willing to bring to consciousness the day's form of action? Art might be written over their prim doors and over the ceremonial bags they held out to receive the public's donations toward beauty, education, and the good life; but the efficiency born of monumental irresponsibility and inertia very promptly applied the means of furthering the good life to the defeat of spirit, the preservation of human pettiness, the toxin of the city. No, it was not so much the artists who were fogging the issues as the aggressively dead institutions.

Later, and again to the accompaniment of indecent exhilaration I saw a little further. It was in the Town Hall. The brisk numbers of Honegger's Symphonic Psalm were indeed very bad. And while Mr. Bodansky zealously fired his orchestra

and exhorted the chorus with summoning stick, and
M. Rothier declaimed his narrative with the superb
old canned unction of the *Maison de Moliere;* and
the *intelligenzia* sat conscious of assistance at an
Event, and effort evaporated leaving psyche the
meagerer, it occurred to me that I was observing a
comic vicarious triumph of the culture-philistines
over old King David. The children of Goliath, it
seemed, have never forgiven the pebble. In New
York, as in perhaps every big city of the world,
they were busy smiting the poor man of God,
lover of the greatness of things, hip and thigh;
quite unconscious of the silhouette cut by them.
Vastly funny, they were, these grotesque shadows
of slight people striving to project personality and
gain significance through business in the arts: exaggerated, unfruitful gestures of men feeling
themselves doing something; actually lost in nothing. Honegger, I am afraid, stood foremost; that
evening again proving himself easily the least generous and penetrating of the serious newcomers.
He is an artist of the sort of those who, while
striking the creative pose, manage to let other people do the main work; providing music that leans
very heavily on literature for its meaning. This
practice procures him easy successes: it has made

[179]

Pacific 231 one of the favorite circus-pieces of the concert room and lineal successor of Danse Macabre by Saint-Saens and L'apprenti sorcier by Dukas. All Honegger is in that piece. Pacific 231 is not a good locomotive. It is well enough made, but it is made of *papier maché*. Or perhaps it is a locomotive in the movies. An out-in-life locomotive makes a much grander concerto starting, steam-beclouded, on a winter's day. The overtones of its whistles are invariably exquisite and blood curdling. There is nothing in the whole world more nostalgic than a distant locomotive crying across a spring evening for its mate. As for the looks of the machine, the giant with the blinding eye in his chest bearing down upon you, no one, not even Jules Romains, has given that, and Hoenegger's impressions are almost pathetically tame. The chorale-like grunt-theme for the brass, and the long mounting violin figure hysterical as a plume of drifting smoke, remain inferior Tchaikowsky; the "sumptuous chords" which gather and arrest the flight of the music are without genius. But those who do not write in the newspapers dote upon the music of Tchaikowsky; and those who do write in the newspapers dote upon it no less, provided it comes to them over the signature of someone supposed to be "modern." Besides, people love to dream on locomotives while the band plays on; so Honegger, by a clever title and clever description, for his perception of quality and color are good, permits them to indulge two loves with but a single stone. And when he murmurs, "I have always loved locomotives as others love women or horses," all allow the intensity of the passion, no one rising to remark that if others loved horses or women as Arthur Honegger locomotives, there would be far fewer horse-races and many more psychoneuroses.

Le Roi David is wine from the same bucket. It, too, is competent illustration done with musical means. No independence of experience in the score. Pseudo-classic modesty. Terse, clear writing, after the manner of the Six; instrumentation done with a musical passman's unindividual cunning with the timbers; the whole making one wonder whether "Honegger" may not be a syndicate, a name under which several musicians publish compositions. Few of the numbers do not reveal Honegger the canny follower, industriously adopting established ideas and processes to the requirements of his text. Few moderns have not used series of low seconds and orientally sinuous woodwind figures like those of his introductory measures; few have not set dissonant trumpets against each other in depicting a military camp; and most have done it better. The best effects of the symphonic psalm are clever rather than moving. The ululation of women's voices in the Lament of Gilboa pleases the ear, and the March of the Philistines with its jazzy brass is heavily humorous. The clock-like tintinabulation of the celesta in The Dance Before the Ark contributes a charming archaic flavor; the whole with its little fugued battle pieces, etc. suggests a pseudo-classic steel engraving. The dependence upon literature none the less assures it a success like that of Pacific 231, and a sensational career for the psalm is to be anticipated at Welsh eisteddfods and other provincial Protestant assemblages where music functions to provide opportunities for the indulgence of conventional religious sentiments.

It must have been during the music that the matrix of the whole great show became plain to me. It was the city: in sudden comic despair, I saw with what completeness hunger for self-certitude had fastened on me during the last hours, and how it had arrived. All day indeed it had been closing on me, the measly strait-jacket of self-feeling, binding me ever closer to myself until I touched myself and

myself alone. Around me there had appeared hordes
of hostile exclusive individuals. And in the midst
of them I had felt solitary, defensive and opposi-
tional. Sitting at lunch, sitting in the club library
over the table of periodicals, I had been conscious
of shrinkage and the collapse of the ground beneath
me: the past and its developments. Nothing had
been said, by anyone. All had been most friendly.
But it had come over me that I was not considered.
There was no censure: still the indifference signaled
that all had not been impressed. I had arrived nowhere with my work. There was no doubt but that
my ideas were exploded and my style uncouth. I
was forgotten, that was plain. But I was not yet
dead! Were only a certain article of mine out, they
would look up! My mind had fumbled for inflam-
mable literary material. I had told myself I must
hurry and do extraordinary work, definitive in
form.—Twenty-four hours had done it; twenty-
four hours of the city and its rootless, jumbled
being. Measly self-awareness, self-palpation, defensiveness, were the form of its disorder and alien-
ation from earth and her cycles. The rapid incessant crowds coming against one like blows brought
it, and the incitation of the leaping ambitious sky
line, and the frantic squabbling for place on a tiny

spot. A city-full of skyscrapers crowding to base themselves each one on the tiny site where It was, where It alone was, and striving to rise alone through the forest of pressing rivals and outshriek them to heaven in line and dome and steam, echoed five million tiny potencies desiring to stand on It and to deny the rest; from the silly intellectuals preening in the prints to the working people on the streets. The people disposed the place and the place in turn disposed the people. To avoid this disconnection from life, then, I had hesitated coming to New York; not because of the oaks regal and ruddy over the fields! They had been mere symbols of the freedom of the heart where ragged chains of hills and out-spreading skies, and night and cold and color lift the burden of his life from the individual, and make him conscious of forces beyond himself. No doubt there were people living quietly, steadily at this very hour in New York for whom the seasons, and the breathing of earth and all the impersonal processes of nature through which man grew and found his peace were evident through mountains of building stones, down slits of sky, and in air vitiated by millions of lungs. Certainly, men would eventually live in cities as in nature, sympathetic to eternal rhythms and stretched beyond themselves. There were purplish rainbow nights when it was possible to look down on a New York waiting with prodigious building masses, Aztec man-made mountains like altars and like headless gods, and sign-illuminations floating loose in mid-heaven, and feel its summons to an individual able to think in terms transcending his own person. But as I reëmbarked on my train for the hill and the lake under mountains, and the old things favorable to man, I knew that for myself and most of my fellows in this generation between the old soil and the new, a day spent out of New York was a day of living music.

EMANUEL CARNEVALI'S BOOK

I KNOW several people carrying A Hurried Man about with them, passionately nosing among its glossy pages: devotees absorbed in the leaves of a little holy-book. I know people who'd prefer parting, for the hour, with almost any volume on their shelves rather than this slight single one of Emanuel Carnevali's. There are not many perfectionists among them, the folk getting a marvelous quickening through the little miscellany of stories and addresses, poems and book reviews. Perfectionists will find relatively little in this piously edited collection on which to pasture a preternaturally exquisite sense of form. Carnevali was only twenty-four years old when they shipped him from Chicago back to Bologna broken with encephalitis; and it was in an adopted language that he had made his things. He was already sixteen years of age when he ran from home to America in 1914. During his few years of creation he handled prose, narrative and critical, somewhat more successfully than verse; and half his relic is in poetic form.

Rest assured that the Poet has some part in cherishers of the splendid tatters of this strangely checked career. A Hurried Man is large, warm, piercing stuff, purest expression of sorrow in American letters. Set beside this fervent writing, affecting like a sincere cry or the grasp of a pleading hand, it is so direct and humble and open, the sorrow permeating classical American literature reveals itself no sorrow at all, but absence of feeling: in Hawthorne "fatalism, hopelessness, moral indolence"; in Poe, weariness from non-living, and morbid voluptuousness. Poor Carnevali's sorrow was warm and born of desire. It was a state transcending the personal; a resolution of individual tragedy in lyrical knowledge of many human lives; a sympathy with forces beyond himself restoring to the individual his primitive harmony of being. Yelling, weeping and cursing in adolescent intolerance, Carnevali none the less managed to release, even in undeveloped bits of verse and prose, feelings about the whole world. Hence it is not alone with the mass of contemporary publications that this paperbound booklet has no connection. Uneven and incomplete, it demands comparison with prose æsthetically delicate, bodied and finished like Hawthorne's, verse absolute and Chopinesque like Poe's.

The great current of life flows out through it.

Besides, A Hurried Man is our expression as few books are; fixing a reigning mood, defining a general state. It is the expression of homeless men. Content, pathos, form where it is active in the quasi-confessional narratives, were found by Carnevali through the types of the unrooted soul adrift in every American city and corner. Four or five significant variants of nonconformity speak richly and accurately through him. He knew the rootlessness of the poor imigrant, struggling for adjustment to a bewildering, indifferent, steely America; and the painfully unstable feelings of the adolescent, outgrown the mothering home but still unripened for the world; helpless, and hemmed in by the brutal contradiction of life as it is dreamed and as experience will have it. The days of the nonconformist for whom the "home' 'is an inadequate reality, or none at all and overfilled with old bones, were equally familiar: days of rebels suspended in the gaunt ways in which neurosis stalks between a family mind and another, future, still shapeless one; days of gods or inferiors eager for Mondays and holiday closings, for the reason that on Sundays and fête-days the fat specter of the old home parades and lies that "the world is a garden of happy children and they are bugbears." Carnevali felt almost grandly the pain of the pitiful sinister types unable to maintain any human relationship; expressions of the restlessness pervading America and all portions of the globe where ancient tribal ways and sanctions agonize, and men wander in emotional uncertainty. And in one incarnation or other, whether that of the immigrant or adolescent, nonconformist or neurotic, the homeless man is ourselves.

Like the literature of the world to-day, American prose and verse is haunted by him and stirred by attempts to seize and to express him. Carnevali's comparative success flows from the fact that for him the rootless and divided individual and his homelessness and unending insecurity, constituted a point of contact with a reality more universal than any of the individual incarnations of rootlessness, or the lot of them taken together. Child of old Europe, this artist knew a helplessness at the heart of life. His own circumstances, pain, squalor and loneliness involuntarily became means to understanding, keys to many weary tragic people: broken women back in Italy; half-crazed workmen in his Chicago tenement; "the homeless, the orphans, whores, pimps, poor spinsters, poor bachelors, homosexuals, young stenogs who won't make good, waiters and doormen, the useless and the strangers"; Dante, Rimbaud, Carl Sandburg; themselves marvelous and terrible incarnations of the dolorous ever-present principle of creation. Perhaps grief had long waited in him, and Italian blood and the Italian past predisposed him to its catharsis. Certainly, religious generations had made possible this humility, this selfless sympathy, not soft and weak, but large and tender, solving the impasse of life and precipitating the harmony with things that renders sorrow melodious. It is only after centuries of religion that a Jules Laforgue can say, *"Donc je suis un malheureux, et c'est ni ma faute ni celle de la vie!"*; or an Emanuel Carnevali paraphrase his cry in racy, vehement, nervously constructed verse and prose. Those centuries have not yet come for the American, or only spasmodically. Spoiled child of fortune, he knows only his own life and personal tragedy; and *that* is like to make him merely boil at the universe for singling him out for crucifixion. Hence, the resentment of personal disabilities, disguised as social propaganda, which fills American books; and the pictures of beautiful souls leagued against by heaven: "saviors" strung to the crosses of Main Street. Hence the marvel of Carnevali's book: the wonder of pain and frustration turned directly upon American soil into sad, exultant, piercing music of a singular purity.

For while sorrow was the ultimate form assumed by Carnevali's feeling, purity was the projector, merging emotions in feeling and making it fine; marrying it to language, driving and refining the expressions till they grew singing and simple and deeply affecting. Every line of his smashing, vociferous essays, poems and stories, has this unmixed, telling effect, clarity of things which have absorbed an uncompromised interest and carry a meaning fearlessly into the world. Instinctively, purity early revealed Carnevali to himself in the sympathetic attraction of the poems of the Others Group, Kreymborg, Saphier, Williams, Bodenheim and Lola Ridge. These clear artists, serene and disinterested beneath their "suggestive violentism, capering simplicism, voracious hunger," passed the spark to the immigrant boy, waiter in restaurants, teacher of Italian, translator for J. E. Spingarn, loafer and husband at nineteen; affirmed the pure creativeness by their own shy example. Le Chanson du Black-

boulé is the Carnevali of the Others period. Later
in his own brief adventure, during his Chicago
years, Carnevali's freshness brought him into conflict with the somewhat sour æsthetic of the exquisite group. He felt apathy behind their aloofness. Two of the five Others sneered, he said; two
of them cursed; and five of them did nothing at
all. "She is a tough-handed and strong-smelling
Woman," he wrote of Poetry in his attack on
Pound; "and rather the crudity and bombast of
an earnest beginner, rather all the pathetic attitudes of self-glorification and self-abasement which
incomplete artists daily pester the world, than the
sophisticated love towards Her, this great Woman
who slings, in passing, streetfuls of dust of to-day's
cities, and whose favorite perfume is the loam.
Rather morbid and talkative love than this un-
gainly *nouveau-riche* abstinence for fear of clum-
siness; rather coarseness that is tender-hearted and
foolishly weeps and foolishly laughs, than the delicacy and aloofness achieved, or rather striven for,
without drama." At this time Carl Sandburg was
the infector, his frank pathos stirring human, pas-
sional deeps in the obligingly tolerated devotee:
and if there is question of a major literary influence
in Carnevali's life, the award must go to the gentle

old troglodyte of the Chicago lake-front. Through what Carnevali called the "song or scream coming to free verse to-day since an image of a Great Hunt became song, song of to-day, song in the ears and song in the throat of a man whom one may see, living and looking sad, as one goes to the office of the Chicago Daily News and asks for the 'journalist' Carl Sandburg," he learned to recognize the superiority of the desire to speak for all the world, the desire to set free that part of himself which was most human, most general. Through it, he was emboldened to finger ardently, patiently, for the pithy, plastic term and phrase, and to search boldly for them amid slang, colloquialisms and the "splendid commonplaces." Always conscious of the material feeling for words, and attracted to the language which colors and models and builds, he came to use common language, "wayward gab" of workers and criminals, and fresh ways of speech, with something of the keen amusement and fineness of the dreamy "motherly" old Swede. Yet in the moments when Carnevali came most closely to being "the voice for the big sorrows, seeking for himself and begging," his cries and imprecations and avowals of love combined a purity which Sandburg never quite achieves, with the pathos and raciness common to them both. Who in America ever spoke phrases limpider than those that came so readily to the vociferous, excitable Italian boy? Emily Dickinson perhaps; and still, it is with a unique pleasure that one comes across the phrases clear as a child's regard, like those in which Carnevali sang his Dove, symbol of his brief wedlock:

"Ah, you are a little darling cloud descended,
  descended to prove to them that clouds may be held
  in our hands and caressed, as though
  they were things of our own, of a tissue alike to
  our flesh.
Dove,
with your red claws like
a frozen lean flower.
Your breast is so soft
that human fingers
might die there,
Dove."

But it is hardly strategic to tear such lines from their contexts. You must turn to the book itself to give them their chance; particularly to the prose. The poetry is fragmentary; auriferous gravel; forcefully sincere and filled with gamey phrases and lyric notes; but ultimately weakened by the absence of rhythmic balance and general outline.

Prose found Carnevali freer; drawing from him in critical pieces his robust contempt of modern American writers wanting love or ecstasy or drunkenness; in the three Tales of a Hurried Man his great tenderness and pure human feeling. The essays are clarions, especially the smashing arraignment of Pound, and the long amusing harangue of the Others. The three stories have the form lacking in so much of Carnevali. Actually *written*, they belong to high literature. Here Carnevali is at the center of his pathetic subject-matter, casting forth words and cries, rhythms and phrases, expressive as those of people caught in sudden crises. The old human pain he felt in women, weighing through them on him and the world, comes marvelously, like a sad and solemn laying-on of hands, through the alternate prose and verse of the first tale. The second, the story of the lame gray dove, gives very subtly in half-pointed, unsentimental phrases, the feeling of the lover, knowing his own love inadequate, and powerless to prevent the collapse of his marriage. Hybrid form, half poetry and half prose, is in its way no less successful here than in the old cantefables or in Heine's Harzreise. The third of the Tales, called Home, Sweet Home, is Carnevali's most elaborate, daring and definitive production.

It reaches a general state through the complex, solid definition of a very particular one. Those twenty-five pages of vocal, milling, extravagant prose render extraordinarily the feeling of the tenement, immigrant, rooming-house existence representing also to-day in their conflicting movements and expressions of gnawing insecurity: sudden florescences of joy and glory out of dolor and downwardness; equally sudden wiltings of positiveness into grayness and perceptions of squalor; atrocities of nerves and agonies of the lost son in the chaotic lodging, the new world. For the friend of American literature they are tragic pages indeed. A very brief period elapsed between the composition of this story and the two preceding ones. All three appeared within a year in The Little Review, Columbus of so much of new American life. Yet the development exhibited by Home, Sweet Home is amazing. The author was leaping into the future; and one cannot read the story knowing what the future actually brought, without grieving over the extraordinary temperament sterilized by disease.

It remains, emblematically. Hear William Carlos Williams: "Emanuel Carnevali, the black poet, the empty man, the New York which does not exist—I celebrate your arrival. It is for you we went out, old men in the dark. It is for you that the rubbish stirred and a rat crawled from the garbage, alive!—What do I care if Carnevali has not written three poems I can thoroughly admire? Who can write a poem complete in every part surrounded by this mess we live in?—His poems will not be constructed, they cannot be. He is wide open! He is black, speckled with flashes, but he is wide, wide, WIDE, open. He is out of doors. He does not look through a window.—We older can compose, we seek the seclusion of a style, of a technique, we make replicas of the world we live in and we live in them and not in the world.—We salute you!"

Written in 1919, more perhaps in recognition of a man than of a work, this rhapsody no less admirably distinguishes "A Hurried Man." Sufficient of Carnevali passed into his book to make it stand where he fell. To-day, the book interprets The Poet to poets, flaunting splendid fragments and tatters that mark our apathetic habits so many dirty rags: so frankly and largely, so utterly without false pride and shame does it record the sorrow, the passion, the cry releasing a man, touching eternal matters.

SCULPTURE BY GASTON LACHAISE

ABUNDANCE lies about all sculpture by Gaston Lachaise. Bellying molds of somber marble, nickel,
and bronze pasture the eye on gravities and ampli-
tudes. Swollen volumes, proud progressions of lines
and planes fill the hands with weight and the breast
with surplusage. The feelings widen to comprehend
these fugues in brass and gardenia-like deployments
of stone form. Fresh with the happy touch of
hands, an hundred shaggy and polished pieces com-
pel with variants of ecstatic rhythm the presence
of the hours when wheat-fields, bodies, and orchards, city towers and star-white nights, ex-
uberantly show the spirit of the cornucopia.

The lumps lead on the feel of having, so daringly big in proportion and puffed into globes and
sturdy cushions, sumptuous, drum-like and mountainy masses. Dilated forms are normal here, set
elegantly against their monstrous fellows or boldly
packed upon them. Each rotundity appears to gen-
erate another often larger companion, or find an

[198]

answer in a rival. Portrait-busts and statues, both, billow deliciously with these complexes, in the fine balance of the pigeon.

Slender and rectilinear volumes intersperse and offset the spherical ones with austerer values. A relatively narrow cylinder almost mechanically regular will connect and balance two complexes of voluptuous forms. Lachaise will simplify the legs of the peacock, the poor feet of the modish woman, to the end of expressing their exceptional meagerness and constriction. He begins a combination of the astringency of archaic sculpture with the soft opulence of certain Renaissance marbles. That is the stratagem of fecundity. The amplified mass and its emotional value obtain through the contrast. Among the rims binding and describing these full-sailed metals and stones abundant like Diana of the Ephesians but all breast, the excessive line prevails, undulant in profound continuous curves and sumptuous ellipses; sometimes opposed and held in by sharp and vehement strokes and edges; more frequently counterposed in grandiose rhythm with lines of its own tendency.

The light caught by these characteristic pieces independently stirs the sentiment of profusion. Relatively cruder and garish on nickels and brasses,

calmer and fatter on marbles, it invariably lies in
warm streaks and patches, bounded and offset by
belts and crescents of shadow equally rich. Pools of
it are permitted to stand by the normal breadth and
curvature of planes. The singular elegance with
which Lachaise contrives to incline, space and join
these surfaces simultaneously invites the condition
of the light, and massively reinforces its suggestion
with the lesson of the progress of superficies. In his
happiest works they swell and depart from each
other freely and gracefully as planes in the bodies
of peacocks, leaping porpoises, and certain mature
and pregnant women. The development is gradual
despite their enormity and boldness of relationship;
marvelously unbroken from toe to crown. The oppositions are clear of violence and pomposity. A
climax is elegantly upbuilt and as tranquilly re-
solved again. There is an ecstasy in many of these
forms, plotted by a sudden twist and intensification of the rhythmic line, a spasmodic impaction
of volumes, a gradual augmentation, kidney curve,
and final tower. Vehemence and nervousness of motion are far. The dialectic of planes and volumes
synchronizes with the steady effusion of the horn
of plenty, ever replenished by deep springs.

It is a fecundity, the principle persistently en-

SCULPTURE BY GASTON LACHAISE

gaging Lachaise, dictating the articulation and flow
of his sculptural volumes, close indeed to the old
heathen *Abundantia,* and still propitious to ideal
existences; and underlying both spiritual and physical phenomena. It is the laugh of the universe,
bearing not only grain and babies, but the leap of
the porpoise, the glitter of granite, the dignity of
the human stride, the brow of the poet. Present
in everything as a breath, it makes the rocks pregnant and fills the world with light; nor does a
novel balance in a beloved human frame potentially
contain more of it for this sculptor than the uncut
stone. One of the fortunates able, no matter what
the conditions among which they find themselves,
to feel the wonder of the infinity of releases persistent in life, Lachaise knows unending cycles of
conception and birth in thought and things; slow
sure manumission through experience; development of power in the individual and the race; inevitable establishment of feelings and ideas solid and
lovely as the material shapes in nature. It may be
too that the vast quantities and sums of new world
life, the profusion of the cities and the spiritual potentialities latent in them also give him, the Frenchman domiciled in New York, an everpresent stimulus. Only, to this day, Lachaise's ardent sober sym-

[201]

pathy with abundance has crystallized most frequently and most decisively through the subject of the mature, nourished and harmoniously fulfilled woman. An hundred of his sculptures and innumerable drawings portray her, in the proud flesh, in contemporary costume, shrouded and rapt in the hieratic pose of the Syrian mother-goddess, carried ideally aloft by her partner, proudly unveiling, striking hands above her head like cymbals, recumbent on earth like everlasting hills, shapeless as a seal and fluid and boundless as the ocean. There is not a little appropriateness in this prevalence of the symbol of the woman who has borne and gives to the whole of life. All that is felt as spirit and indwelling force was once the expression of a countenance, the flotation of a hand, the balance and the rhythm of a bodily port. It is the woman that first gives the artist the experience of ghost and flesh become one flower and a material transcending both. And whatever its immediate incentive, all feeling has the tendency, even when circling through interstellar space and binding immensities, to direct itself toward the typical being which integrated it; and at frequent intervals to find itself in a love-poem, and the state of a world in the features of a mistress. Besides, there is a seasonableness

in the image of the woman fulfilled in giving. The
present conception of the relation between the
sexes, consequently the present æsthetic and religious orientation, connect with it. That connection,
that orientation, are generous, anti-ascetic and affirmative. It is the overflowing being we hold vir-
tuous, and the self-determined, innocent. Relation
requires two positive, equal individualtiies; and cer-
titude is in the sex, to-day, as though all women
were procreant.

Lachaise's sculpture shows of course numerous
happy projections of the cosmic, flowing feeling he
wishes to fix and externalize through objects other
than the grand symbol his work so daringly has
made and continues to make his own. The keenly,
humorously studied penguins, flying dolphins and
sailing seagulls, slender evolving girls and burlesque-
show torsos embody much of his spirit. The man is
an intuitive portraitist, arriving at some of his lightest, completest forms through penetration of the
essential quality of human masks and bodies. His
head of E. E. Cummings is wellnigh the idea of the
Poet, a pressure of two impinging hemispheres
ejaculating divinity and dirt alike through the ori-
fice of the mouth in restitution to the all. The head
of J. Sibley Watson, the *flamen Dialis,* is lumpish

[203]

bronze become sensitive, ennobled and refined at the cost of vitality and active virtue. Up to this time, none the less, abundance has taken to blooming most proudly about those examples of his art stylizing the contours of a woman large, superb and graceful as the letter O.

The art of these buoyant pieces is born of the simplest, directest projection of feeling. Naturalistic observation and mystical brooding both have nourished that emotion; but in incandescent moments it becomes a plastic play. Invariably with the character and pose of the growing object, and the sense of the flight of sculptural volumes, this man of the large, grim, sensuously fresh touch receives the idea of a corresponding consistency and disposition of solid enduring material. Hence, his work is in the best tradition of sculpture, not in Michael Angelo's and Rodin's great inferior ones. It is essentially textural sculpture, conceived immediately as the treatment, the exploitation of a particular medium. These serenely breathing pieces sad with great feeling, address the eye never as flesh or stuff or modeled clay. Each stands innocent of the intention of imitation and visual deception. The contact is made solely through a play and relation of forms in certain varieties of rock and metal. What philosophical ideas attach to the sculpture, are made consequent to the physical form of the rough, veined, and gleaming stuff. Since it is, in many states and variations, the spirit of plenty Lachaise wants to embody, a peculiarly robust quality of material, a grain at once rich and tight, reserved and magnificent, is intuitively preferred. Among stones, the dark-colored, relatively coarse-grained Tennessee marble comes most frequently to his hand. Among metals, his choice goes often to a somber, ruddy bronze, and we sometimes find him leaving the medium in a rocklike auriferous roughness, more frequently bringing it to a high brassy polish, and occasionally contrasting the two states in a single form. The favorite material, none the less, appears to be neither Tennessee marble nor bronze; not even silver "with its virgin hue," but nickel. Thinly lain upon a surface of bronze and made to shine like mirror-glass, it gives Lachaise the textural quality half light and half robust, simultaneously brilliant and resistant, implicit in the great mass of his conceptions.

The execution, too, is of the body entire. No temporary, tentative mold intervenes between the conception and its final form. The stone receives the idea immediately from the sculptor's sensuous mind. He cuts directly in the rock. In the preparation of the plaster model for the metals, the feeling of the whole is permitted to dominate. Individual facets are left to come to life half consciously beneath palms wresting to realize the large, the essential, the "true" form. A long apprenticeship in the inclination and ordering of surfaces preceded this capacity for direct attack on the inner, mother shape. Lachaise is one of those who insist on a lengthy practical acquaintance with the mysteries of the handiwork. Once the great rhythm of the sculpture is fixed, and the progression of volumes harmonious, he will apply himself to the elaboration of detail and development of the little individual planes. Here again is a modern artist unfriendly to preciosity. Indubitably because of his radical method, his sculpture speaks so compulsively to us as work pushed from within, alive with a breadth which seems first to have passed directly to the heart of the crude bronze and stone, then worked itself to the surface again, twisting and shaping the inanimate matter in harmony with itself, and achieving independent being. What transfers itself through the immediate contact of artist and material is indeed a corporeal rhythm, a body's half-conscious balance; in this great instance expanded in the feeling of everlasting fruitfulness.

Since corporeal rhythm involves an amorous yearning for and apprehension of the unknown form-giver of all life, transcendental meanings naturally cling to most of Lachaise's product. Almost all his works might be called The Planet, like the black marble floated on its own basal lines, since the vast number of them to some measure hold the heightened consciousness of the freighted hours when earth with her metal tons, flowering soil, and liquid atmosphere is felt deliciously a-sail in space, sustained on the wings of her own birdlike buoyancy. Or La Montagne, the name of a dark stone informed with the repose of matured women and of hills; since each of them triumphantly holds the equipoise of those mountain nights when the creative force wears the aspect of a gigantic full-breasted woman extended indifferent to man and his petty day; head averted and suffused with dreams of her own ideal ends; and still in moments sovereignly at one with him in common fulfillment. The ecstatic leap of the heart of life is plotted, say, by this fugue in brass; the dignity of human movement in that swelling rhythmic dispo-

[207]

sition of dusky bronze cylinders. The fullness of many individual human masks and frames moving toward union with the all, the spasm of the all as it shoots through many finite forms, calls wonder high. It is the brimming heart, we know, that prays.

THE DANCE OF ANGNA ENTERS

ANGNA Enters stirs shyly before the font from which all issues. Wittily, sharply, reverendly, her serviceable person and costumes represent the unknown form-giver through gestures of women unconsciously expressive, like their fashions, of the pitches and tempi of past times. A sequence of abrupt, discordant and brutal steps and poses combined with the drag of a voluminous velvet skirt and the vicious snapping of a whip, swiftly embodies the dislocated spirit not alone of the Heptameron of Margaret of Navarre, but the whole epoch of Fontainbleau, the Primatice, and St. Bartholomew's night. A series of angular and primitive, heavy and exalted motions and attitudes executed to the Frescobaldi air in a red Gothic gown and diadem, plots the curve on which the cathedral measures the infinite in steep, yawning architectural reaches, suspended in a gulf between hell and heaven. Trailing, elongating, sinuous bodily play associated with flopping picture-hats, droop-

[209]

ing shoulders, long black gloves, hips and trains, creates the blooming "modern" times of the early century: luxuriously appointed capitals, languid intellectualism, Pelléas et Melisande, stock speculations and the Merry Widow waltz. And as the young dancer's grave, humorous and complete little pictures, veritable abstract compositions follow and oppose each other like complementary colors, there hovers, veiled, the great dark bourne mysteriously projecting forms, spirits and times, triumphs, visions and tragic deaths, and as mysteriously calling them back into itself again.

As yet, Angna Enters represents the unknown form-giver more hesitantly than directly, not quite freely enough to permit the hidden agent to show a living visage and affirm the day in the figure of contemporary woman. Her incorporations of the gestures, ports and balances of the sex compose a mimetic history of the world, a book of images from the past, an evocation of what has, most often gloriously, been in femininity. True, her repertory sports one notable, contemporary sketch of a theater lobby during an intermission with a smart woman unconsciously suggesting the "limit" in a series of brittle, jazzy postures. Possibly the little Sherwood Anderson story in pantomime, the ap-

pealing show of the vacuum about the adolescent
girl at the piano, is to be associated with this biting
picture. Nonetheless, these two pieces and others
born of the feeling of to-day are not among the
compositions that place Angna Enters in the ranks
of living art. They belong in the class of her many
slight, caricatural dances: the satirization of the
bourgeois aristocrats of Napoleon's court in Antique à la Française; the unmerciful depiction of the
1917 flapper and her goodnatured dirogations. It is
in the French Gothic Queen of Heaven, so majestic
its balance of ample and delicate gesture, so frank
in its large pathos and larger joy; in the picture of
the Viennese Fräulein opening forget-me-not eyes
and the more romantic apertures of the heart during the dipping measures of a Johann Strauss waltz;
in the angular little Flemish Virgin so awesome in
her red and gold and scepter-like gestures; and in
the unforgettable Tess-of-the-Durbervilles picture
of the peasant girl prancing her candor, fragrance
and trustfulness to the Beethoven *contredanse*, that
Angna Enters is most largely declarative of life.
These compositions with their related play of characteristic gestures, stand among the loveliest, freshest creations the contemporary stage can show;
equally attractive and inventive in conception and

execution. But sacred and earthy simplicities, virtues and generosities; at least simplicities, virtues and generosities as maryolatrous and agricultural civilizations bore them, are not quite immediate; for all the eternal feminine they contain; for all the unwillingness with which mankind sees them removed.

Even shy and hesitant expositions of the form-giver do not lack the power of orientation. We feel a universal through them, no matter how coolly and aloofly it is brought into relation with us; and the dance of Angna Enters has several components sufficiently general and revelatory to affect us, and to suggest its dominant retrospectiveness preparatory to a discovery of the new spirit. Backward looking though it is, her conception of feminity is broad, contrasted, and delightfully antithetical. Besides, the very amplitude and tenderness embodied in the damsels and Virgins, maryolatrous in feeling even though these qualities are, deliver a challenge to the day, incline whatever scale they address themselves to, to balance the world by the production of a corresponding contemporaneous refinement and sublimity. The fact that Miss Enters' mimetic is a medium of direct approach to life, independent of the significancy of music, is

also most important. Her dance creates a form leaning upon that of no composer, rathermore taking
the musical accompaniment up into itself and reis-
suing it. It is music, as most dancing is not: a significant pattern in mimicry, often a little canon, as
in the Queen of Heaven, or the Moyen Age danced
to Frescobaldi; more frequently a *lied*: theme, variation and free recapitulation. Assembling and
forming experience with this independence, distinction and freshness, Miss Enters reconciles the musician to her use of his art, differing little from the
conductor or pianist's creative one. The spirit of the
music receives an extension through a medium
other than tone, none the less closely related to the
musical through the common source in motor activity; that is all. Miss Enters' waltz creates toward
Johann Strauss whose Geschichten aus dem Wiener
Wald accompanies it. Experiencing life through his
voluptuous measures, she invents an authentic
charming counter-point in bodily rhythm, facial
play and ultra-Viennese costuming. One almost
knows the words whispered to the Fräulein extending her arm like a violin, and hopping and
springing with German ardour and romance.

A deal of the miming is done without musical accompaniment. The Dance of Death, with its hec-

[213]

tic trapped movements, dead black dress, dead white face and ghastly wreath of cheap stuff flowers,—it is one of her most satisfactory conceptions —is entirely unaccompanied. Still, musical art is no more servile in the dances executed to Frescobaldi and Debussy, Waldteufel and the unknown modist of cathedral-building times. Angna Enters' art is creative, not interpretive; this sensitivity toward her composers distinguishing her work from that of Isidora Duncan. Save in her moments of preparation and repose, Isidora never fused with her composers, setting them and herself free. The personal isolated her movement from theirs; there was no construction. A great friend of ours accurately observed that while Walter Damrosch conducted the Seventh Symphony to her dancing, it was perfectly evident that neither mime nor conductor was interested in Beethoven. The unlucky Titan strained at the double load. But Angna Enters is a "musician," perhaps because she unites in herself something of the artist and of the woman.

At instants, one glimpses her person in her mimetic; glimmering like a star in a night-cloud; high-shining, liquid, and vigorously bright. Invariably, it is the dance which obtains through the dancer, not the performer by means of the art. Not only is the play of light upon the body and the costumes subservient to the idea. Bodily pose, facial play, costume and setting are carefully considered and inherent parts of it: most marvelously perhaps in the Queen of Heaven and the terrible Odalisque. This impersonality is not merely Japanese and conventional, but spontaneous and devotional; of the priestess not by convenience but by vocation. You are never conscious that it is Miss Enters who is beautiful, even when a characteristic play ideally lifts her eyes. The wealth in the person is given to the dance, rousing the spectator only to the fairness of the improvised temple enclosing him, and to the moment of beauty in which he participates. Like the independence of form, the objectivity of the presentation reaches the universal. But for it, one might be content in calling Miss Enters the new Yvette Guilbert, and letting the matter rest there. The younger woman shares the pertness and levity, the penetrative sympathy for humble manners exquisitely characteristic of the singer of

"The pity of unpitied human things"

The simple and frivolous become poignant objects beneath her mind; and like Yvette, she borrows from the past and is best evoking it. But the larger instrumentality places her engagingly somewhere a little beyond the dry Yvette in the grand direction where Duse shines; exciting us to watch her with something of the deep interest we give those other contemporary men and women fully, immediately, representing the world.

TURNING TO AMERICA: THE CORN DANCE

OUT of Kansas City on the bread-plains, all was familiar to me save the informing gorgeousness. I craned to see the terrifying stretches they had led me to expect on my trip to the Indians. At first the Limited hastened west through apathetically billowing country; but what, ever more pointedly as the day grew long, flung itself by the windows and dwindled down the slender fleeting trackway, was at once the commonest and the most wondrous of American stuffs. New over the Missouri, I nonetheless knew this country. It was past Julys. It was perennial heat, termless platitude; pain of old summers in the corn-patches of New Jersey; emptiness on Long Island, New England, Virginia downs. It was all the ancient barenesses, homelinesses, flatnesses which impotently burdened spirit throughout the land. Kansas had gathered them from out the East; but prospects without accent and roads without events, dirt of tilled fields and detailless greenery and shadeless crops, raw telegraph files, sidings of freight cars in Indian war-paint, clumps of human boxes and sweating threshing-crews, now showed cheerfully, glamorously, gloriously. Concentrated, homerically swollen and voluminous, hot fertile soil, hot bearded grains, hot shining varnish, all that had weighed, opposed and baffled, was full of richness to the spirit; the doorposts and entryways of home.

Why, I wondered, had I gone so long unaware of the loveableness of America? It was the ventral land, the pagan unbroken now! Shameless and sunburned, away from the flying platform, earth spread under a brooding heaven; abandoned to the celestial embrace, breeding tissue, bone and blood from her sweet breast. Babies crawled over her; there was no beyond, no time and space, past and future. One principle only existed in this slow oven of fleckless insistent sky, limitless plain and golden bread between: a perpetual mindless *here*, a single baking station amid wire fences, beneath the steeples plastered with tar-paper. Immanent nothing opened directly from the main streets of the towns with their linings of Fords. Roads sped blankly north and south toward horizon that secreted no otherwheres beneath their rims and only the unchanging fecund present. Yearning could not breathe, was ridiculous, in this dry ocean. If indeed an Ideal persisted, it could only be some rolling god of crust brown abdomen and hot round limbs, an old earthen pot all of a piece. Art that could ripen here would long rebuff our intuitions with apparent monotony, and only difficulty impart its slow deep pulse, close to non-rhythm. Dreamless, the warm bodily life extended, solid begetting, pure survival, procreant earth and urgent sky, the vedic poem of America. It had been boring; it was monstrous still; but it was good for below the little stubborn region of the self where the individual will sat entrenched.

Evidently the westbound track led to clarity. By evening the Limited gained the arid zone, and the new step of siccation heightened sense of discovery and harmony. On the bread-plains, familiar objects had lain in a new light. The imagination had passed from the known to the unknown. The span it leaped in the mountainy desert was wider, more comprehensive, and more robustly affirmative; starting with fantastically strange sensations and finding a profoundly germane core. I had not previously known air that gave no support, had passed through fire and thus grown light and not to be leaned on. Walking hilarious at midnight by the resting train at La Junta, I seemed to breathe

[219]

in pinewoods without scent. Strikingly new was
the morning world, dry, tinted, dizzy; exhilarating
the passengers of the dining car like the pink clouds
over the hard blue rocks, that were lofty mountains. I had never seen a quilt stretched over town-
ships; gaped at a desert stitched by a cosmic granny
out of alternate pink and poison-green patches.
She had also upholstered some crumby slopes in
plucked velvet. It had grown a little dusty with
age. But depravity was at home with her niceness.
Hills were livid convicts branded across their vil-
lainous fronts. Beyond Lamy, the little tamarisk-
planted junction and its tangle of squalid chapels
and houses, the cruel treeless land began, studded
with cedar shrubs, tufts of sage and the writhing
cup-bearing green serpents of the candelabra cac-
tus. The parched wide plateau of colored rocks,
colored sand, gay-colored air, glittered illusorily.
The blue teeth and tusks stuck up in it were Rockies, distant great numbers of miles. The painted
canvas stretched on a jagged low frame-work, and
prepared for the sudden tower of a gigantic show-
man come to juggle oranges, was the remote Hamos
range!

Yet how satisfactory, the otherness! For a first
time, I found mountains tranquillizing. Uneasy,

mysterious appeal was not in these, absent with its parent, the undulant rims of watery lands. Hard as the split blue stones mashed in roadbeds, the stern guardian shapes stood, summoning nowhere. They were; and what was in them was not a degree dearer than what was present, on the slowly mounting roadbed. Moving, going, advancing, could bring you no nearer it. Dryly, austerely, impersonally, indifferently, finally, the geometric Rockies expelled wretched yearning pathos. Life was back in the tight skin, taut and coiled. The whole world, the petrified past and vague future, was present, or visible from this eagles' eyrie; infinitely more copious and referrent than in Kansas. There, the whole world had been provincially contained in the happy functionality of animals; and Europe had been unthinkable. Here, on the aristocratic altitudes, Europe, Sophocles, the Old Testament, the Æginatan marbles, Don Quixote and Stendhal, were real; close as the green Mexicans in the train; great and yet neighborly as the pyramidal summits that were indeed lofty and seemed small of scale. Again, I knew this country; and feeling the grasp and order of the perspective, my churned feeling brought up the name, "America." Midmost the continent, New Mexico lay about me, its penetralia; at once the sacred essential point of the land, where it was most itself; and the mysterious projection of a long dormant idea. I kept repeating, "The most American place," knowing nothing precisely through the words and yet finding expression in them. Vaguely, uncertainly, a concept born of the stark drought, made to assemble a sprawling geographical dimension and a formless human throng in a single shape. But where it lay and what it was, I could not ascertain.

Then it was there again, like the ghost in Hamlet; haunting, half-emerged and provocative, the stage of Santa Fe and its alien, entertaining settings. On the bottom and sides of a shallow dishpan filled with green instead of warm sudsy water; among sand, pinions and orchards, a south-European hill-town stretched its low mud walls; and the feeling of orientation, the intimation that this half mediæval, half primitive place facilitated a grasp and definition of the chaotic thing America, hovered; and even swelled in defiance of divorce from acceptedly Yankee properties. Strong in a Spanish or Italian hill-town, and among furniture (the five alice-blue walls of my rented room were crowded with pious chromos of the Virgin of Guadaloupe in a mother-hubbard, Saint Nino de Atocha with

glebes of corn, and sundry bleeding heads and
hearts of Jesus,) that was itself strongly uncon-
nected with the nervous, fuming industrial fields,
my feeling declared the reality of America only
casually involved with the contemporary habits of
its tenants. Persistent in the face of a Latin people
classically cordial, uncensorious and reserved, it
confessed that reality equally independent of race.
The primitive shapes of the flat, square, terraced
adobe houses flaunting jolly carmine, creamy and
dirt-brown sides, and studded like the face of Liszt
with warty beam-ends, reiterated and showed it
perfectly unhistoric. All day along the Canyon
Road proceeded the comic-opera stuff of women in
rebozos and Ford-compelling artists in ten-gallon
hats, flappers booted and spurred, burros mantled
with cords of kindling, Franciscans in robes and
Stetson straws, mounted terra-cotta Mexicans and
Indians in Sweet-Orr blue. Sunday mornings a
whole railway-depot clanged from the monasteries,
seminaries, hospitals, convents, schools and cathe-
drals; and Sunday evenings a veritable folk festival,
a democratic continental institution assembling rich
and poor, brainy and dumb, progressed about the
band concert in the gently lit Plaza where the old
Santa Fe trail comes to an end. Still it continued

to emerge, the unifying principle of American life; only the final interpretation held back. Various conclusions presented themselves, curiously implicative of a profound, secret hostility in the earth. For a while, it seemed clear that America was a fundamentally arid country, inimical beneath a superficial fecundity to man's existence or to that of his ghost; obstructing the expansion of human life through a cruel relegation of man to the plane of economic struggle. Then, a mysterious kinship with the classic European soils, inevitably necessitating the derivation of American culture from that formed in the Mediterranean basin, suggested itself. But neither properly composed my jumble of austere, serene and tragic perspectives.

The mutter of a war-drum, the static maneuvers of the phalanx of a pueblo dancing for corn, at length brought clarity. Possibly an extreme of physical experience precipitated it. The August noon concentrated furious heat and drought about the Indian village of Santo Domingo. The low tenements in the broil of sun foundered in sand. Sole greenery, the fringe of cottonwoods along the stripling Rio Grande might have issued from a Noah's Ark. The motor had to be abandoned in a mound of granular bake. We had to wade through

a kiln of parching air and sand to where people
stood massed on the roofs, and the monotone of the
drum arose. The crumbling treeless plaza of the
pueblo swam gaseous with heat; then an unknown
force responded to the excess and found it good.
Crowding under the rude whitewashed porches
filled with Indian men, women and children; in
among tourists, chauffeurs, anthropologists, con-
sumptives, schoolmarms, soldiers, buds, boy-scouts,
Harvey busmen and other relatively fatigue-hued
whites, my friends and I found ourselves transformed into framework for an amerindian rite.
Distinction of race dwindled. Whites and all wore
appropriate costumes. Colored fabrics in the audience grew articulate, jazzy; the ladies were all festive; and his striped shirt and handkerchief with
which he had awninged his hat made even the most
commonplace male bird gay as a woman or an
Indian. For the moment, no ritual was in progress.
The file of dancers circled through a temporary
shrine of singers in the near end of the dusty little
plaza, genuflecting before an altar piled with
loaves and glinting with candlelight. Then, the votive procession straggled and disappeared. Suddenly from the far end of the place where it had
gathered, the bulk of brilliant bodies and orna-

ments, of bronze, white, green, blue breasts, of
robes and chains and hair and branches, launched
toward us in a slow, steady, shaking trot. Without
tension or development or resolution; monotonous,
warm, unfailing, a living drumbeat, and short iter-
ated human cries, possessed the air; pounding regularly as the heart; at infrequent irregular intervals like the heart missing a beat, and drowsing the
brain with the throb of sheerest being. Tufted with
red and yellow plumes, steadily dancing up and
down in piston-like rhythm, a tall pole in the two
hands of a rose-shirted brave led the ritual; occasionally bowing over the all-mother ground in
the gesture that is at once fertilization and benediction, then resuming its steady grave mechanic
play. In a moment the space before us lived with
insistent sound and motion, and the regular repeated pattern of tone, of color, of gesture and
movement, a kind of multiform fugue in the monotonous brute idiom of Moussorgsky, embodied
the process of plant and animal and human growth.
Sprigs of blue spruce were pointed ecstatically, iter-
atively, toward the dry heaven, by the closely
massed, gaudy, filleted, chanting elders of the orchestra. Mute and impassive, suns and moons, the
human pairs trod and gyrated continuously before

them; strong summery color. The man led; round naked bronze to the waist; sprigs of spruce flaunting from each of his biceps; a knot of aspen leaves atop the flowing mane. Ropes of turquoises, white deerskin kilts, trailing white furs, white cuffs and hooves of stuff, completed the magnificent impersonation. His dance was a slow, regular, hopping trot; a positive relentless stamping. Close behind, danced the woman, with movements markedly discreet, passive, and receptive toward the man's; her corpulence, her tall hieratic headgear of heaven-blue, her woven black dress, and brown hands extending branches of the spruce, admitting and resolving his action and supplying a ground and counterweight to it. Through the indefatigably bobbing ranks that gyrated now in pairs and now in sixes, single, naked, braves dog-trotted: Koshare, smeared ghoulishly with white and ornamented fantastically with corn and gray feathers. These were ancestral spirits supposedly invisible to the dancers; present here as in every great act and art, and stimulating the dance with their wisdom. Slowly unwearingly, relentlessly, the groups of twos and sixes pattered past each other, penetrating the body of the dance. Unbroken the furious drumming rolled. Unflaggingly the tree-like pole bobbed, and showered the mother with blessings. Gaudy in its sateen shirts down over cotton pants, the orchestra sang and gesticulated toward the coming shower. The dog-spotted ancestors described their fantastic arabesque. And whenever the rhythm suspended a beat and then struck again, the entire body of orchestra and dancers synchronized accurately with it and changed gestures and footing as a single performer.

Their round maintained a station. Weaving, vibrant, pulsant, from its inception every passage of the dance contained the end. Divided into alternating groups, people of the winter and the summer, each with its donjon-like kiva at an end of the place, the performers unflaggingly continued the formal idea in the drowsing monotony of recurrent figures. Only the lengthening shadows varied its face, till sundown, when the two peoples merged from their opposing kivas and as one principle rounded their dance in the swift dusk. Long previously, while yet members of the one or the other unharnessed group, atop its adobe dungeon, made brilliant spots against the drop of fawn-colored sandhills, the immediacy, the abstract presence of America was plain. A moment, still, the blissful monotone of the related media, and the gratification of feeling a form, a rhythm, take up one's personal life and America, and hold and objectify them, were points in consciousness. Feeling, about myself and my friends and the visageless undefined numberless throng of compatriots was curiously fluent. Then, in electric clearing, accidents and persons vanished; and round the pueblo the whole intra-oceanic stretch, and the past present future millions upon it, stood, a monumental immobility. It spread, America, no place of becoming. Solid as concrete, the moment extended underneath the sun. There was no death; there was no sundering birth. "The shapes that were gone were here": ancestors and unknown æons; and individual surcease left no fissure in the tremendous mass. Being, not becoming; pure timeless being, was the secret unifying principle of this continent as of all other dry and classic soils. The solid, long, level chant of Whitman knew it! Only along its coasts did this land resemble Europe, swimming in mists, seas, rivers, rains. The mighty rest was Mediterranean, volcanic, desert, a zone of statuesque station, of fixed forms and immutable types; and traits of its general stationary, unchanging character permeated every inch of its earth; seaboard downs and coast-wise ranges no less than midlands, prairies and plains.—American for twenty thousand years, the red man's cognition of basal forces, and hymn and thanks to them, plainly communicated; timeless station and rejection of the lone-star, self-feeling individual. Bodies were his instruments, but the piece they executed was rich with feeling of a great single communal life mounting in earth and crop, beast and men, in unison with the sun. Willingly the many conflicting American perspectives composed themselves in harmony with his knowledge. To the east across the plains the tall New Yorks shot up, turbid flames of self-assertion, towering ambition, ceaseless becoming; for an instant offering to give the lie to the Indian. There, as never before, was change, ceaselessly mounting and melting sky lines, frantic competition between buildings and between individuals each of them It. But from this southwestern perspective, the restless becoming seemed hollow, the mere accelerated spinning of unapplied wheels on a derailed locomotive. The motion was external, broken, nervous. There were no individuals; and the frenzy of the tall New Yorks seemed merely the resistance of the inherited racial rhythms to the spirit of the new world. Born of the perpetual modulation, the inevitable individualism of the Faustian north of Europe, and rooted in neither

[230]

old or new continent, what had once been cosmic
yearning now expressed itself in senseless motion;
and what had been the assertive romantic ego now
lived on in the degenerate form of insatiable personal wishes. Ryder was more plainly than ever
the poet of this phase; his ghostly Flying Dutch-
man, Death on the Racetrack, Jonah in the Flood,
the form of dynamic longing only nebulously connected with earth. Still, in those jumbles of granite
fire-works and virtuosic spiritual display, the great
American cities, what curious adumbration of the
logical norm, the type! What suggestions of embryonic order in their architectures! The Shelton,
the Telephone Building and the other organic
piles!

For a minute, then, my conviction weakened.
Was it the vision of the other, industrial America
that undermined it? Perhaps; for with the fume of
chimneys, the black of factories, collieries, grinding masses, I felt a shaping, unifying process bearing down on me indifferent to value and feeling,
destructive of what would not join in its self-
loving business. Oh yes, it mocked at me, regimentation was in progress! Still, by what feat of fancy
could standardization and industrial regimentation
indifferent to quality in life, to the value and pur-

pose of existence, neither releasing human forces
nor realizing the possibilities of the marvelous land
herself, be considered anything but a miserably inadequate response to what in the soil called for social imagination and a communal culture? Could
anyone prove that rootless individualism and the
American earth were commencing to collaborate?
A few buildings, a few artists? I remembered how
many democratic ideals were languid, how universally Americans ignored and lived indifferent to
quality in things and people, how busy their civilization was with whip and bribery, forcing external conformity onto the world. They saw nothing; and whenever had human beings so wanted
dignity and interest? Yes, indeed, regimentation
was in progress; but a civilization based not on
feeling but half on rigid theory and half on mean-
ingless mechanical proficiency could never free men
or warm the daily life with vision. And what was
to produce the organization of the elements of life
in the form of culture? Certainly not a lot of un-
practical people like the Indians and ourselves, the
handfuls alive to wonder. Over such, America
loved to glide like a steam-roller. Were we really
more than discards even now? Poor Indians dancing for corn, and otherwise poor audience of neu-

rotic whites and half-poets, anthropologists and curiosity seekers—what rôle did they play, and what
could they play, in the big society successfully interested in a standard of material comfort?

Could one bank on the influentiality of the soil?
What the red man danced, what in his unadvan-
taged way he lived, was the thought of the soil; an
agricultural conception initiated primarily to mo-
bilize the village at harvest time against marauders,
secondarily to incline nature to man by adjusting
him to her conditions; by way of these two serv-
ices having become the work of art, the religious
ceremony, significant to the red tiller of the purpose and value of his life. But our existances floated
above a "soil." From the beginning, our society
had had a tendency to dissociate itself from the
earth, and its product, feeling. The puritan had
ever striven to rise above the soil and escape it; and
industrialism had finally fulfilled his wish.

But the dance once again pulled me up. Before
me, proud impassive people trod their round, beautiful in summery color, sure of foot, living on,
saluting the four ends of earth. The black locomotive of America vanished. After all, there was not
so much to fear. In industrial America as in all
the world there was merely soil and man, lean-

ing each on the other, both working together and living together. Through men, the crops and waters; and through the earth, man and woman in their rounds of sun and moon. Here, besides, was a machine, made of women and men, bobbing up and down like a piston; not dancing with a cruel machine-like beat, but with the rhythm of human beings. Were they too not bound together, men and earth and the machines, by the desire of men to live, by the desire of machines to live, perhaps by earth's desire of florescence? None could exist independently. They were bound to come together, and harmonize. To function perfectly, would not the machines have to synchronize with the great rhythms pulsing in the air? And what was it that reached up in man, little cunning grandiose man, so free with his old mother, but the forces that shaped the earth he trod on? Those forces would find him again in his cities, entrenched behind his granaries, notwithstanding the artificial heat and light of electricity; and he find them, when security and leisure once more heightened his appetite for experience. Love would no longer be for personal delectation; but for the feeling of the whole of life: as now before me.—What the new communism would resemble, whether it would be a new feudalism or a new bolshevism, and whether the great corporations were initiating it, could not be prophesied. But it was inevitable and welcome; since through it the intuition, the cognition that gave this serene, level Indian dance of Kansas and New Mexico and the whole intra-oceanic stretch its form, would reappear, in the new white America. Yes, when the soil and man and the machines were in relation; and style pervaded all the manifestations of life, art would top man's day like a temple-dome; receiving his excess and renewing it once more. A last time, I looked at the Indian rite. The immanent future was in this ritual of a dying race! So the new Americans would dance, with the racial past, the cruel sun and sand, beautiful about them through acceptance. And at that moment, the chant of the war-drum and the Indian voices, the regular leap of the static phalanx into the vertically striped sunset, was not so much the expression of a pueblo affirming tribal unity and dancing for corn, as a kiss: the spirit of a country calling through a vanishing old lover to another perhaps just awakening to her beauty, perhaps not even born; summoning joy of certainty and offering him life and a prime criterion.

THE IMPORTANCE OF RICHARD ALDINGTON

THE title must appeal ironically to all who have been irritated by the gentleman's leannesses. They're not to be overlooked; Aldington is wooden, of the second strings. In spite of the international literary adventure in which he's participated, he remains a kind of Englishman of letters. There is even something of the masculine old maid about him; vivid currents, moments and imports turning so gingerly at his touch. You cannot with the best of wills place him on a level with Eliot, Pound, H. D. and the rest of the epoch-making poets of war and post-war London, whose companion he was and whose innovations he appreciated. He is as far behind them in sensuous responsiveness as they as a group are behind D. H. Lawrence in fire. Nonetheless, it is not possible to read his excessively *soignée* poetry, so dainty in its form and fine in its expression, and not receive an impulse and feel a personality. It embodies an idea, thin as its play may be found to be; an idea of aloofness, of detachment in stuff and handling.

Aldington has had what in his best Greek manner
he calls "an intuition of the unalterable gods." Of
course, the Greek manner, "Phoibus Apollon," "the
Kuprian's breasts," "Kimmerian dusk" and the rest,
are a trifle insipid; summoning to mind an Oxford
student in a tunic being corybantic according to
the books. But the poetry does lie in the line of
things; is "objective" and lapidary. Aldington's
verse is imagistic, metaphoric; composed of crisp
figures in several sensuous fields, chiefly in the
visual; and the workmanship is as precise as the
material. Laxness of line remains nobly foreign to
it. Rhythms and verbal combinations echo

> "The brief shrill clang of glass on ice
> The note of fragile metal sharply struck."

There is a keen tactility, our finger tips continually
running on rims acute as

> "the line of near hills
> Cut out in thin blue steel
> Against red haze."

A world has been caught in action. The movement
is unfailingly serene and impersonal, subtle with
hesitation and pause, and controlled by the will to
"gather something of repose—some Attic ges-

ture." The war's very introduction of harsh notes, pain and sensuality, does not break the detachment; and the hardness of matter and exactness of workmanship, the slender sound and firm handling, compensate for absent *brio* and authority.

Which immediately suggests the importance of Richard Aldington. An Oxford student in a tunic, he has none the less naturalized "pure" American poetry in England. He was the first of his countrymen to recognize the value of the experiments of what has since been discerned to be the most important contemporary movement in poetry; the first to refresh his art with the new vision. That vision, of course, was of a pure, a self-contained poetry which, "free of loose relative reference, using symbols without association outside the literary range of the poem itself, and effective through a great technical rigidity," would lean on nothing for its meaning, and be thinglike, lapidary, objective. The experiments made in sympathy with it moved in a direct line toward those uncompromizingly "absolute" minor masterpieces, The Waste Land, The Comedian as the Letter C of Wallace Stevens, and the Sordello-like Cantos of Ezra Pound. Perhaps because of its references, the adjective "symbolistic" ought to be adopted in place

of "absolute." The movement of Pound, Eliot and
Company had its counterpart in France during the
nineties, in the group surrounding Mallarmé; and
in Germany during the nineteen hundreds, in the
group about Stefan George; and in both instances
it was called "symbolism." True, during his London heyday, Pound attempted to father his school
with an obscure English wit named T. E. Hulme.
(The maneuver resembles that of German naturalism, which, inspired by Ibsen, sought snobbishly,
unfilialy to ascribe itself to Hebbel.) The American pure poetry movement in fact is the expression
of scholars versed in French literature. Not that it
imitates continental models, for all the Laforgue in
Eliot, and Paul Fort in Amy Lowell. It is attribut-
able; to the abstract tendency in modern urban,
scientific, mechanical civilization; having analogies
not only in the contemporary literature of many
lands, but in the arts of painting, sculpture and the
novel. (Even music has recently turned from romantic descriptivity toward self-contained, absolute conditions.) Its imagism, figurativeness, besides,
is preponderantly visual, while that of Mallarmé
and Kahn is musical, chiefly; and its sensations like
its metaphors are of its own discovery, part bookish
and part metropolitan. Still, all of Pound's group

have been students and in instances translators of
the French symbolists. Symons, whom they enjoy
badgering, they read: "If we can recall the time
when we were ignorant of the French symbolists and met with The Symbolist Movement in
Literature," candidly writes T. S. Eliot, "we re-
member that book as an introduction to wholly
new feelings, as a revelation." They talked with
Yeats; Jean de Boschère, latest offspring of the
Parisian magicians, was associated with them in
London; and the accurate future will doubtless
know them as the first American symbolists. So,
if in this note on Richard Aldington's conciliatory
rôle, we persist in calling the group he naturalized
in England poetic absolutists, it is merely for the
purpose of insisting a little longer on their vision
of independent poems: forms, creations, things
complete in themselves.

Aldington's fullest embodiment of their principles is to be found in his phantasmagoria A Fool
i' the Forest. Previous to the time of its composition, and since his commencements as a pallid, post-
Swinburnian atticist, invocation of the Greek divinities and all, he had developed into a full-fledged
imagist. The direction was Pound's. We would like
to think Aldington more the collaborator than the

disciple, since so little in his adaptations is slavish. He is always personal; beneath his constant stylizations, one invariably meets the mind of the English gentleman struggling to face what the day has brought his world, and preserve a manly sweetness amid the crass decay. No question but Aldington learned for himself from his patterns, as he has learned from Landor, the Athenian choruses, and the Restoration lyrists. But A Fool i' the Forest scarcely bids us call him free at forty; no more than his earlier poems; even the vignettes of the war. If the little work's reliance on rhythm, phrase and image as the chief agents of meaning, is of the time; as rightfully Aldington's method as it Pound's or Gertrude Stein's, Joyce's or Hart Crane's, the use to which he has put it, the significations he has bodied forth with it, are scarcely original. A Fool i' the Forest is another Poem of Doubt, an absolutistic work in the spirit of the famous Cantos and The Waste Land. Undoubtedly, what made Pound and Eliot write their minor masterpieces was likewise at work in Aldington. It must have been the Englishman's own disconnection that originally drew him into a group whose common characteristic was unconnectedness. Pound, Eliot, Stevens and Company are not mere minor poets. They are major poets out of whack, twisted and balked by unwill. Almost oriental in their sensitivity to their material, concerned for daintiness of shape and fineness of expression, leaders in the exquisite advance of poetry, they front life neither robustly nor steadily; most constrainedly in comparison to D. H. Lawrence, their major contrast. There is a deal of sheer "Can't, oh!" in Pound's Draft For the Beginning of a Poem of Some Length. While their poetry has epigrammatic succinctness and delicacy of rhythm and expression, it quite lacks fire, warmth and gusto. It is cast in cool, oblique, ironic forms, and much of the sarcasm seeks out the author's egos. Fragmentariness mars some of the liveliest of their attacks: Pound almost never rounds out an idea, and Eliot, more successful in his shorter pieces, fails of giving "The Waste Land" the unity necessary to its prosperity as a work of art.

In any case there is nothing vicious in the circumstance that like several of his group, Aldington should have applied his most ambitious and sustained efforts to the production of a Poem of Doubt. The Poem of Doubt remains an ultimate expression of his group, much as the poem of passion and weariness of passion (Cynara, The Sphinx) remains the ultimate expression of that of the or-

chidean nineties. Unwill, conflict, defensiveness
commonly takes the form of painful suspension between the equally positive poles of affirmation and
negation, and attachment to passive suffering. Objective reality, so seductive to the passions, appears
simultaneously insignificant and treacherous to unwill's weak, uncertain lights; unsteady, unpleasur-
able, offering only the cheerless choice of shipwreck
on the ocean of adjustments and starvation and in-
sanity in the waterless waste-land of unrelation. Of
course, the war and the peace were prolific in justifications of tragic stinginess. Hence, the smoky
funeral pall lying on the "London" of Eliot's great
poem of doubt, the feeling of falling worlds,

> "Jerusalem, Athens, Alexandria,
> Vienna, London,
> Unreal"

the brutal miscarriages of lyricism; despair assuming the parodistic jerks of jazz; and the ignoble
couplings half amusing, half torturing the poet's
mind. Hence, too, the rôle played by the war in
A Fool i' the Forest; the despairing conclusion in
the picture of adjustment to the world purchased
through betrayal of the inner man.

But while expression through a poem of doubt

may have been natural to Aldington, his is no improvement on Eliot's which preceded it; nor on Pound's, brilliant and meaty for all its emptiness, important for all its asininity, which preceded that. Not that the faults of The Waste Land, for example, are minimized by those of A Fool i' the Forest. They remain evident. For a piece of absolute poetry, of symbolism, for an interplay of forms and qualities of rhythmic, verbal expression, Eliot's poem leans too heavily upon its notes. Its unity is disturbed by too great a quantity of themes, consequences of the poem's undisputed origin in several distinct conceptions. The perhaps necessarily languid and ironical tone wants adequate relief. And then, T. S. Eliot is a genius who is also a very clever dog, a bit of a smart-aleck à la H. L. Mencken or E. E. Cummings; for which reason he never quite succeeds in ridding us of a nervous distrust. Nonetheless he is a very gorgeous poet, minting gold from the psychic alleyways he haunts. His rich, mordant and melancholy feeling for words, his choice of macabre images, recaptures some of the wormy magnificence of the characteristic pages of Donne and Jeremy Taylor. Invariably musical, The Waste Land at times achieves a

native stateliness of movement "the violet hour
that strives"; and is most effective in its dramatic
oppositions; its twisted grand, romantic, affirmations of life; its ironic realism; dislocated style part
bookish and part colloquial; and all the other expressions painfully lyrical of rootlessness, and tragi-
comic indecision amid kaleidoscopic vistas. The
sense of London communicated by the poem is extraordinarily rich; it is to Eliot and James, more
than to the contemporary English, that we must go
for perceptions of the spirit of the monstrous, sinister, matter-of-fact place. With The Waste Land,
as with the Cantos and The Comedian as the Letter
C, a full symbolism made its triumphant entrance
into Anglo-American poetry. And if any piece has
the chance of living as the lyrical expression of the
state of incompletion, as a poetical equivalent of
Ulysses, it is this.

Now, A Fool i' the Forest is anything but a poor
poem: the "gemlike cutting of the Greek" invariably delights in Aldington. The little work's outline is clearer, the material more unified, than that
of The Waste Land. An amount of this unity may
be due the circumstance that Aldington is telling
a story, recounting the adventures of an "I" and

[245]

several symbolic characters from the Commedia del Arte, and may therefore be superficial. But an equal amount is due consistency of purpose. And where Aldington writes directly, permits himself simplicity and gravity, his phantasmagoria is really moving. There are portions of it as poignant, sharp and delicate as the best of his earlier pieces and The Lover in the Images of War; and the motives displayed in Exiles, his immediately preceding volume are developed in it. The rising of the moon on the Acropolis, the Landor-like lament for youth, the midnight patrol (one of the succinctest evocations of the war) and the funereal vision of sleeping London, with its "million breathing corpses," belong among the achievements of the recent literature of precision. Not, alas, the irony, the romantic parody, the sardonic realism, distinctly derived from Eliot, and wanting Eliot's verve and fine diablerie. To be sure, Aldington is exquisitely appreciative, a cultivated intelligence in an eclectic age; a respectable workman. But irony is distinctly not his vein. Eliot's handling of his second-rate material, the depressed and mocking voices of psychic conflict, was first rate, happy and inventive; while Aldington's dislocated moods, acrid turns of language and rhythm, despairing parodies of Campbell, Byron,

the liturgy and American advertising, are wooden
in comparison, and make one feel the Englishman
of letters.

Which once again brings us to the ostensible
subject of this harangue, the importance of this secondary author. Is it not precisely in his secondari-
ness that Aldington's consequence lies? In mediat-
ing, attempting to integrate the experiments of
the verbal relativists with the tradition, has he not
put his minor gift to uses momentous for both
American and English letters? On the one hand,
there was a number of rebels; on the other, an old
tradition. The rebels were disconnected, psychic
exiles, strangers in more than a strange land, and
the tradition was decadent, dying with Hardy, de-
teriorating with Bridges. Doubtless under some personal necessity, Aldington stood between the two,
unconsciously interpreting them to each other,
making what was racial in himself understand the
new feelings, and harmonizing them with his ancestors' religion. In thus combining them, in vivi-
fying the old English feeling and belief with the
new American daring, he was not only furthering
his own heritage. He was corroborating a band of
experimentalists in their own direction, and assuring them of a wide influence. Pound and the rest

must be deeply indebted to the welcome and understanding given them by this gentleman in whose
blood the culture of old Europe ran. Not alone
Pound; was it so long ago that word went about
New York Richard Aldington had said, "the best
English prose is being written by Americans to-
day"? And do not the Sitwells and the other English experimenters who have learned so much from
the Americans, stand in a direct line behind this
English officer of liason?

That office is probably terminated to-day. The
air is full of rumors of a polite revolt. First, there
is the essay somewhat belatedly saluting D. H. Lawrence, a great author quite outside the exquisite
tradition and continuously denied by Pound and
snubbed by Eliot. Second, there are some ominous
words in the essay on DeGourmont. Talking of the
use to which Huysmans and Villiers de l'Isle Adam
put the confiding young critic, Aldington stops to
say "Nothing is more unfortunate for a young and
inexperienced author than a strong influence from
older authors who have failed, either as men or
as artists. I have myself seen a writer of some promise ruined by an uncritical admiration and friendship for a disappointed senior who imbued the
young man with all his personal enmities, all his

whims and fads, all his feelings of bitterness against the world. With the candor of youth, the young writer accepted discontented grumblings as sober facts; and with the reckless generosity of youth, made this lost cause his own." *Prenez garde, Messieurs les meteques!* Another man has grown aware that there "is a certain type of literary man who lives in inverted commas; drinking port because Tennyson did, a Tory because he is endeavoring to apologize for his Middle Western origins!" Perhaps this is the commencement of the complete Aldington, influenced at last through his American relations by the Declaration of Independence? We hope it is; simultaneously aware that a spontaneous Aldington would merely augment the respect coming to him now, as one who has lent his person to a fine experiment.

SACRED AND PROFANE MUSIC

IT has become essential to recognize three distinctions in the music of our time. The first, opposes mechanistic, metallic, relatively uncolored compositions, of the sort of Strawinsky's and Varèse's, to earthy, homely nature-poems like the symphonies of Sibelius. Divergence here is not so much a matter of the difference between an architectural and a descriptive music, as of a difference between the thought of city mouse and country mouse. One kind of music is citified—megalopolitan in best (worst) Spenglerese: the form of a life relatively independent of seasonal change and vegetable growth, and sprung from the mind of man. The other is agricultural, product of man's ages of harmony with the slow cyclic process of the world and dependence on water and crops. Material aspects very appreciably contrast the two sorts. The sound qualities are dissimilar; those of the first, harder, more precise and less vibrant, in the character of metals and concrete; those of the second looser and softer, in the character of sky and soil and waters.

So too the rhythms, prevalently rigid and iterative in the one, more irregular and cumulative in the other. Varèse is non-colored, Sibelius iachistic. Both musics are the forms of orders existing confusedly in us, one less and the other more familiarly; the first probably a waxing and the second a waning, root-feeling.

My second schism spreads through music from another direction, and reawakens echos of a famous æsthetic feud in the Paris of Marie-Antoinette. Again, Piccinists and Glückians battle over the nature and conception of music; we have, side by side, composers holding their art an independent phenomenon to be practiced only in reference to itself, and appreciable only to a refined superficial sense; and composers relating it directly to the sensibility, the passions, and the understanding, and addressing with it the union of faculties called the mind. Under the hovering spirit of Satie, Strawinsky and the young Italian, Rieti, lead the clan of those striving to satisfy themselves with formal relations and movement in itself. The leaders of the poetical party attempting to express the cries of ecstasy, fear and despair through unusual harmonies, broken melodies, unprepared changes and violent transitions, are to be found in Glück's

[251]

native Vienna, about Arnold Schoenberg. The grandfather of the new Piccinism is none other than M. Camille Saint-Saens, purveyor of emotive fragments of inferior interest. His letters abound in axioms like, "Art is for the purpose of expressing beauty and character. Sensibility only comes after, and one can do without it very well." "Form, loved and cultivated for its own sake, is the principle and very essence of art." "The pursuit of expression is the germ of decadence." "The more sensibility develops, the more music and the other arts depart from pure art." Modern Piccinism, however, bases itself on a misinterpretation of the architectural impulse of contemporary life as well as on a misinterpretation of Bach and Mozart. Persuaded that architecture follows the lines of an "objective" necessity, it seeks to build music on these lines; forgetful that architecture is distinguished from mere building by the presence of mind. It is to be prophesied with some confidence that the restoration of the world-feeling damaged by the war will put an end to this and similar conceptions born of weakness.

The third distinction in the contemporary musical attack, became plain to me during a performance of da Falla's new little concerto for harpsichord. The other two arrived more gradually; but the last dawned on me with all the suddenness of an adventure. Still, as I look back, I see that a couple of anterior impressions prepared a terrain favorable to it; the earlier of these having been given me by Kaminski's Concerto Grosso for grand orchestra, the latter by da Falla's tripartite poem Night in the Gardens of Spain. The German's composition struck me as startlingly opposed in spirit to most of the music made during the last century. True, it is not without kinship to solemn passages of Wagner's like the prelude to the third act of Die Meistersinger and the polyphonic pages in Parsifal. It is even more closely allied to the music of Reger, of Bruckner and of all the archaicizing German moderns; and something of its spiritual nature is to be attributed to its uncompromising polyphonic, elaborate and baroque form and style. Kaminski in this score very deliberately aimed at a "further development of Bach's polyphony by the contrapuntal treatment not only of single voices but also of different orchestral groups; by a working together not merely of melodic patterns, but of rhythmic and harmonic as well." The scheme of this piece for double orchestra with piano and percussion is indeed "an immense elaboration and extension of the classic orchestral form of Bach and Handel." In place of the classic concertino, Kaminski has used a duplex concertino of string trios, and his conception of tonality is modernistically liberal. Yet this return to the methods of the early eighteenth century does not alone account for the æsthetic quality of the concerto. That, is both newer and older than the spirit of Bach and Handel. Listening, the night of its first New York performance, I realized that its Gothic severity and characteristic combination of massiveness, and of sentiment divorced from sensuousness and married to unearthly solemnity and ecstasy, constituted a new birth and a fresh category. If the excessive feeling of mass and weight was modern, the grinding and ornate passages for woodwind, the darkly colored volumes, and the strident angular final fugue were deeply racial, deeply *Teutsch* and metaphysical. More uncompromisingly than Bach himself, Kaminski set me amid the aspiration of Gothic arches in the unearthly twilight of a northern church. As the orchestra played, I had the impression of tapers staring from out the darkness, and an organ moaning of doomsday.

Still full of the German work; a few days before hearing da Falla's harpsichord concert, I had found

da Falla's Night in the Gardens of Spain directly
opposite in spirit; as wondrously involved with
palpable things as the concerto had been sheerly
upward-streaming and unearthly. I had heard textures of satin and of flesh. In the final section cellos
and horns sang afire with elegant melodies and relaxed, slow-breathing rhythms delineative of the
body's immortal poses. Brilliant and nonetheless reserved in the Spanish temper, orchestral iridescence
disclosed the strange pricking earthy timbers of
the instruments, tasting of oranges and nuts; oily
and tart together. Arabesque in the first section,
In the Generalife; popular and brutal with its
gongs, shrieking violins, and stuttering, shattering
trumpets in the second, Far-off Dance; sumptuous
and lyrical in the finale, Night in the Gardens of
the Sierra of Cordova, the music sang the earth,
and concluded in the tone of the easy rapture and
happy eloquence that glorify the elegance of the
flesh and the whiteness of starry skies. And yet this
composition, worthy follower of Wagner and Rimsky and Debussy's sensuous pages; and art of the
sort which twenty years of experience of the concert hall have accustomed us to think of as fundamental, on the December days on which the Phil-
harmonic performed it, no longer was exclusively

central. Not that it dated; or that its indebtedness to Rimsky—the young Prince and the young Princess from Scheherazade expire in one spot of da Falla's score—detracted materially from its magnificence. Its orientation was merely plainly one of two; and the marshalled evidence of the third division spreading athwart contemporary music, began urging a conclusion.

Then, at the concert of the Boston Symphony, while Mme Landowska and the accompanying flutist, oboist, clarinetist, violinist, and cellist sounded forth the churchly music of the second movement of the da Falla harpsichord concerto, the conclusion descended. The simultaneously dry and tinkling sounds had evoked a candle-lighted eighteenth-century interior. A *concert spirituel* was plainly in progress among lace ruffles and abbatial black; and it was quite easy to see that to-day again music has fallen into categories of sacred and profane, spiritual and worldly. Only a little while since, we could all chime in with Walther von Stolzing answering Kothner's query, *"Wählt der Herr einen heil'gen Stoff?"* with *"Was heilig mir, der Liebe Panier, schwing' und sing' ich mir zu Hoff!"* But to-day we have a double beauty. Doubtless, the churchly, the purer and more perpendicular feeling is present in Parsifal, and in passages of Franck and Bloch. But it was still fused with the profaner, more horizontal and outspreading feeling; and it is only through the ultra moderns, Kaminski and Webern, and in individual works such as the harpsichord concerto of da Falla and the Three Choral Preludes for Organ by Roger Sessions, that it has arrived at its old independence.

"VOGEL ALS PROPHET": ALFRED KREYMBORG

ALFRED KREYMBORG figures in the field of modern art as a prophetic bird or vocal, feathery sage. Wisdom, of which he has not a little, is one for him with imagistic verse, drama and prose of a decided, light, capricious musicality; and work of his in all its stylized forms puts one in touch with life in the detached, tender way called wise. The world has not frequently had the opportunity of feeling as acutely through so puckish a music.

Extreme reliance on tone as the prime agent of meaning from the very earliest set him apart from the great body of imagists, the band of modern poets persuaded like himself that poetry is a continued metaphor rhythmically organized, the communication of a state of being through visual and auditory figures. Rhythms seen do the major work in their verse. Kreymborg, however, for all his dryness, essentially is one of the poets like the German Schiller, creating out of "a musical state of soul." The sly meaning, message, state of being his work is there to communicate, reaches us most fully through its tone-patterns, rhythms, lilts, cadences.

[258]

No matter whether it is formally to be catalogued
as a poem, a play for marionettes, or piece of au-
tobiographical prose, the best of everything he has
produced remains fundamentally a tiny tone-poem
or music-drama, composed for an æsthetic Uber-
brettl or inspired vaudeville. Gestures, movements,
costumes of the actors as well as the words of his
playlets themselves, are conceived in terms of this
pitch-rhythm. The beat of the players' soles on the
boards are as strictly controlled, as metaphoric, as
legitimate embodiments of some invisible significance satirically shadowed forth, as their dance-
like, clock-work statements. Small wonder then
that in the opinion of Waldo Frank, Kreymborg
even more than Eugene O'Neill deserves the name
of founder of an original American theater!

Visual rhythms, too, have a good share, play
important and well-sustained rôles in Kreymborg's
charming toys. Striking from him as from all the
rest of his imagistic band a fusion of figures in
several sensuous fields, experience has found him a
fine variety of fresh personal visions, perceptions
and subjects from out the fantastic jumble of
modern American life. Many of these are city-
motives. Kreymborg is one of the authentic minia-
turists of New York, experiencing life through the

commonplaces of the mad high town, finding in
the articles of a five and ten cent store, in animals
in the zoo, in pushcarts, toy-balloons, street-organs,
summer-night moths, garbage men and giant spikes
of steel, a poet's witty, sophisticated points of contact with the whole. One of the chief delights of
Troubadour, his sensitive history of his first forty
years, is the richness with which it recreates two old
New York City atmospheres. Were the delicate
book bare of other charms, which it most positively
is not, these evocations alone would amply in-
gratiate it. First, there is the picture of the old
German-American New York up on the middle
East Side. No copiously documented description
after the manner of the naturalistic novel, it gives
form, trait by trait, to the poet's childhood environment; until there spread about us the arid
leagues of asphalt without a tree, relieved only here
and there among the rising buildings by an empty
baseball lot. Central Park is blocks away to the
west, but there is the third avenue "L." And we feel
the easy tribal life, accented here and there by an
antagonism to Irish America personified by a pompous landlord or school-superintendent, but unaware
of conflict with an American idea. We experience
again the vain resistance to the march of industrial

organization which, beginning in the late nineties, finally drove the small shopkeeper to the wall; hear the good-hearted German-American jargon and the good-hearted folksongs; see the chess-players in the tobacco shops; and eat German pancakes for Sunday morning breakfast.

Then, as the narrative, novelistic in its suspense, passes to youth and early adulthood, another New York background comes to life; very different from the simple, slightly airless first; equally unhandled. We have had many romantic Greenwish Villages. But before this one we have had no veritable picture of the incubation period of the new poetry and art in its shells about Fourteenth street. Kreymborg's autobiography shows us the years when the generation of democrats which is printed to-day in every living magazine, exhibited in every living dealer's gallery, and advertised on every living publisher's list, froze in hall bedrooms and tiny studios, roasted in Grantwood shacks, hung up at bakery lunches, and listened to editors lecturing them on the wholesomeness of American life and the ideality of the happy ending. Indeed, the book unrolls something close to a chronicle of New York's bohemia. The birth of the free-form movement, the first battles between the adherents of a petrified conventional poetry and a personal, rhythmical one; the arrival of new recruits and the shaping of instruments, publications, little theater movements; the gradual reception of the survivors of battle, are suddenly historical matters, filling a space, hitherto nebulous, with distinct contours and shapes.

Even more decidedly than the excellent local colorist is Kreymborg the moralist; profoundly concerned with the relations of human beings. It is startling how frequently, despite crypticism and indirectness, for half of Kreymborg's method is understatement and obliquity of attack, this discreet, chirping fowl is to be heard warbling of love. Heine himself is not more guilty; but Kreymborg is more humanistic than the bitter-parodistic German. The point is, he neither romanticizes his feelings nor the objects of them; having a sympathy for people as they are. Indeed, beneath his apparent benevolence, mildness, and "shyness," there resides an acute critic of human nature. While the main achievement of Troubadour, say, consists of its atmospheres, a scarcely secondary one lies in the keen, significant little vignettes of the small regiment of figures who have shared in the author's

private and professional careers. Beginning with
Father and Mother, done with the tenderest filial
feeling, elusive as mist and yet solid as rock, the
historian passes on to the equally fairly rendered
images of the three women in whom his intimate
experiences centered. Then come the companions:
Sandburg playing catch with a nickel ball in Chicago; Marianne Moore discussing the "respective
technical merits of Pound and Aldington" on the
way to the polo grounds and then criticizing like a
fan the plays she had only theoretically known;
Stieglitz talking and actually being out-talked by
Roosevelt at the famous 291 lunch table; Bodenheim arriving from the west to meet the man "who
seemed to have the elements of friendship in him";
Dorothy Kreymborg being cajoled to drop her
"shyness" and play a little Mozart on the piano.
Indeed, almost every one who has figured in the
artistic life of present America is touched off by
some characteristic trait, however minute: Ryder,
Anderson, Mark Twain, Dreiser, Hartley, Scofield
Thayer, Man Ray, Pound, Eliot, Williams, Stevens,
Frank, Frost, Robinson and many others. And
while at moments one fears that the book is about
to begin to read like the city directory, the fear is

unfounded: Kreymborg is most appreciative of people, and his little words have well-considered meanings.

Hence perhaps the moralism of his verse and theater, the humanistic reasonableness of his love-poems. Of recent years, notably in the sonnets, Kreymborg has tended to embody his experience and knowledge in a music more elevated and oro-tund than the light and puckish one of his first volumes. Still, the rhythms continue to affirm de-tached, unassertive relationship to things, and re-main half tender and half ironic, uttering the child and the old man in unison. The poet is per-haps the American Massinger: his individual tone lying so justly between high music and flat prose. And whether he chirps and dances, or attacks straight narrative, we find him "small" in his charming way. This slenderness of Kreymborg's, "capering simplicism" in Carnevali's phrase, has frequently been misunderstood by his public, will-ing to read into it a refusal to come to grips with life. No interpretation could be further afield. Kreymborg's moderation is, first of all, humanistic, and secondly, truthfulness to the scale of life nat-ural to him. While he stands opposite the great ro-mantic affirmers of present America, say the group

about Alfred Stieglitz, he too is neither rational-
istic or sentimental; merely an artist of a dryer, less
passionate cut. On its scale his experience is a complete one. If the maturity of understanding at the
root of his verse, the birdlike affirmation of cultural,
amorous values is not sufficient proof, there is the
testimony of "Troubadour" to corroborate it: in
spite of its shadows as confident and happy a record
of the artistic adventure as any other American
autobiography. No, Kreymborg has lived and
grown wise expressing himself and what in present
America is related to him. And the production of a
sagacity that is musical and a music delightfully,
humorously wise assures him not only a perch in
American poetry, but in the great wood of the
world's literature.

COPLAND WITHOUT THE JAZZ

THERE's a new colt in the American pasture, all legs, head and frisking hide. You may call it Aaron Copland's musicianship, if you like, which however won't prevent it cantering past you on long uncertain stilts at your next encounter with it; the body oddly small in proportion to the motor-power; the head huge, and as wooden and devilish as that of a rocking-horse. It's an amusing affair, in the incomplete assemblage of the organs, limbs and twinkling skin of the racer; charming with the awkwardness of the large young thing not long from the mother. Impressive, too; since it's so conspicuously the colt of American brass and momentum, of all that is swift and daring, aggressive and unconstrained in our life; slender blood-brother of the new architecture and the other constructive flights of the bold temperaments.

The "legs" immediately point the pedigree. Copland's music is decidedly kinetic. Wistful or burlesque, it has taut instinctive "go." His most characteristic, ambitious pages are spasmodically motory. The hiccoughing rhythms of the scherzo of the symphony and the allegro of the concerto beat jerkily, insistently, with mad mechanic joy; as though unwilling to cease before a world were involved in their breathless, iterative patterns. The young composer is prolific of polyrhythms, and piles them up under emotional necessity. And whether his music balances itself to slow three eights plus five eights, or careers over roofs to the same three plus five tremendously quickened, its structure of abrupt changes under high speed embodies something familiarly, natively American: climatic, social, mechanical, one scarcely knows which, it is so general.

The "head" corroborates the "heels." If Copland's earlier compositions, the ballet in particular, occasionally prove insensitive and prolix, even the most jazzy, inconsequential of his recent, representative compositions, say the violin pieces, are beautifully governed, ingeniously put together; while the major exhibits, the symphony, the suite Music for the Theatre and the concerto, discloses the presence of a practical, resourceful mentality. Things in slender beaten brass, these pieces are sheer projections, products not only of a rare sense of the elements of music, but of an equally rare capacity for conceiving compositions coolly in the terms of

the technical problem. Copland brings us inter-
playing tonal forms, significant metallic structures
lightly, lucidly joined. Romantic as some of his
shafts and girders are, hot-colored and exciting not
only with garish jazziness, but with all sorts of percussive, brazen brilliance, the great interest of his
music nonetheless remains the architectural one, the
interest of the independent, projected, self-sufficient object. In their bareness, essentiality and faithfulness to the line of strength, his tonal edifices resemble steel cranes, bridges, and the frames of skyscrapers before the masons smear them with mere-
tricious stonework.

What has not yet matured in Copland's musicianship appears to be the capacity for a dedica-
tion of power with an intensity proportionate to
its size. If we see the musicianship in the irreverant
form of a gangly young colt or sublime daddy-
longlegs, it is precisely because of this hesitancy of
an important pathos and expression. The body;
indeed. What amazes us in this youthful New
Yorker's work is largely its prodigious snap, brilliance and burlesquerie, the tastefulness of the
material and method. But these are superficial features; and the quality of the inward elements, of
the music considered as content, speech and idea, is

not exalted. Not that Copland is to be censured for avoiding the affirmations and objectives of the past. Certainly his fragmentary, sardonic moods are more realistic, truer to the world's state, than any mere recapitulation of Wagner or of Brahms could ever be. Nonetheless, they leave us dissatisfied. Copland stands to-day one of the most independent, able and promissory of the new American composers—Roger Sessions, Carl Ruggles, Carlos Chavez, Roy Harris, Adolph Weiss, Ruth Crawford and the rest—and one of the country's engaging artistic figures; but the meagerness, not so much of his musical methods, as of his impulses and aims cannot be overlooked. Indeed, he may be said to have only two tempers, and to swing regularly from one to the other. The first, a rather plaintive, wistful one, a mood of early April afternoons, gray clouds, gurgling frogs and perhaps a single, always single, blackbird, has contributed the first movement of the symphony, the third of Music for the Theater, the violin nocturne and the introduction to the concerto. The other, a wild, cackling state, full of machinery madness, the old cat and fiddlesticks and the lunatic moon, is the progenitor of the second movement of the symphony, the second and fourth sections of Music for the Theater, the violin

[269]

serenade, the choral setting of Pound's An Immorality and the body of the concerto. And while both have produced happy pages, respectively sensuous and airy, and champagne like and overtoppling, neither is direct, fervent and aggressive. Both reflect more of a racial past than of a present. Both are eccentric, disjoined halves of the unified, deeply swung state called feeling. The one is nostalgic, the blues, the other, parodistic; and jazz.

Copland's grandiose jazzing is not without pungency. Frequently it transcends the merely satirical and muscularly contortuous, and approaches a kind of releasing, Rabelaisian laughter. Without question the spirit of his profane, satiric setting of Pound's Immorality is preferable an hundred fold to the calfish, pathetically unimmoral vein on which our Dante conceived his little song;

"Though rose-leaves die of grieving"!

But on the whole Copland's jazzing does represent a compromise with a slack, inexpressive, part mechanical and part externally satiric, attitude; and constitutes the scrubby side of the composer's otherwise healthy relationship to the popular modes. The fair one is his artistic, expressive use of

the typical jazz polyrhythm, most beautifully ex-
emplified in the slow fox-trot beat of the inter-
mezzo of his suite. No doubt this compromise with
the cheap spirit of the moment was inevitable, the
form of a greensickness scarcely to be averted. It is
none the less to be deplored, particularly since it
threatens the permanency of such, in other respects,
admirable pieces as Music for the Theatre, the violin
serenade, and even the clangorous magnificent
piano concerto, perhaps Copland's most attractive
composition.

Meanwhile, the coming "body" throws its shadow
before it. By no means Copland's most successful page, the last movement of the symphony is
none the less his most noteworthy, suggestive as it is
of the line his advance must take. Written, significantly, to gather and resolve the contradictory
moods of the preceding introduction and scherzo,
characteristically nostalgic and mechanic, it also
makes to embody the whole-feeling, reconciling the
two eccentric halves of a personality; clearing the
road for its development. True, the form of this
finale is stiff. It has neither the elegance nor logic
of that of the plaintive introduction and the hiccoughing scherzo, and leaves the symphony half
suspended in air. For all its abrupt transitions and

lumbering volumes, nonetheless, the movement reaches and touches deep stratas. Motory, clear in its outline and net in its structure, brazen of tone and impetuous in its beat, it neither mocks nor yearns nor jazzes; holding instead a state of being that is of our swift mechanical civilization and yet somewhere free above it; and converting ruthless, relentless action into an agent of beatitude. Here in embryo is the style and feeling related to our noble colt's long legs and head; a brief of the freedom toward which Copland's musicianship seems desirous of advancing. And with an authority no other page by Copland can match, it reaffirms the earnest of a composer, able to balance American life in running architectural form and spread its relish rainbow-wise over the earth.

THE AMERICANISM OF CARLOS CHAVEZ

STRICTLY on the external plane of things, Chavez's recent piano sonata and ballet The Four Suns, persuade in their precision, architecturality and green reserve. "Classical," they do not embody a return, like the precise, architectural and "pure" composition of the Strawinskies; or lean on theories; or preach existing orders and societies in musical terms. Where the great mass of their European companions and competitors merely chill and disaffect, these most characteristic works of the sturdy young Latin from Mexico move by an eminent involuntariness and virginity. Undeluded, bony and dry as his own high deserts, and peppery as chilis, sonata and ballet constitute a veritable classic music: form and expression of commencing cultures.

They attest all his pieces works of an incipient Adam de la Hale, Josquin des Près or Haydn of the fresh American world. To be sure, the half dozen estimable productions of Chavez's probationary years, the sonatinas for piano, for piano and violin and piano and cello, the songs on the poems of Carlos Pellicer, and the racy little improvisations called 36 and Horse Power, ingratiated themselves no less immediately than the maturer pieces as independent attacks; necessary, progressive, and bright with Latin gayety and unceremoniousness. They gave New York the surprise of finding their native Mexico City not at all the provinces and "down there"; and a perfectly contemporaneous place on the edge of the future. Music was developing through someone named Carlos Chavez, it was evident, as spontaneously as through contemporaries in New York or Paris or Vienna. The man was himself an environment. Reminiscent of Ravel as it was, the compact, forceful little piano sonatina moved in a deeply affecting primitive singsong, Amerindian in its rigidity and peculiar earthy coarseness. The droll dry little piece called 36 furnished some of the slack, debonair and crude-colored music, the vaudeville, "from Missouri," art which the Parisian Six set out to create in their brief heyday. While Horse Power was scarcely unprecedented—symphonic works woven of favorite Spanish and Spanish-American rhythms and tunes are common products of the musical ferment in Spain and Latin America—this piece of popular inspiration was nonetheless distinguished by its prodigious snap; its loud good humor; the brilliance of its elevenths and thirteenths; the shrilling reedy clarinets; brittle, percussion-like pizzicati; and the thoroughly contrapuntal treatment of orchestral timbers. Several omens of the mature classical style of the sonata and the ballet, appear in these six or seven records of the rising steam. The completeness with which The New Fire, the very early, still very dainty and Debussian forerunner of The Four Suns, eschews pistorialness, is significant. The sonatinas are architectural, modal, simply polyphonic; and play in strictest time. Sere effects of tattoo-like themes and precise staccato volumes abound in them, particularly in their many scherzo-like passages, and throughout the little 36. A beautiful form of Chavez's habitual suspensions, so accessory to the plasticity of his music, occurs in the third bar of the piano sonatina, in the arrest of a bit of three-part counterpoint in quavers on a sudden crotchet. Indeed, if the intrinsic classicism, aboriginality, of the composer was not immediately recognizable, it was merely for the reason that the immanent spirit had not yet become clearly and decisively fleshed. While the general style of Chavez's precursive works is not imitative, it is not decided, either; lightly recalling not only French impressionism, but German romanticism as well. The first and final movements of the massive clamant violin sonata are fairly Brahmsian in their thickness, rich simple harmonizations, their rolling rhythms and solemn lyricism; while the slow movement a little echoes the loud languorous call of the nightingale which warbles so passionately in the ninth of Schumann's Etûdes Symphoniques.

The ballet and sonata however address us in language whose musicality is not too apparent at the first shock. The medium's unvoluptuousness, precision, bare structuralness and the closeness of the textures, let them appear wellnigh inexpressive. The singularity of the shapes, *abrutie* and squat as Toltec divinities; the abruptness of the transitions and rhythmic sequences; the frequent teasing suspensions, arrests and hollow octaves, seem the pitch of willfulness and illogicality. As a matter of fact, acquaintance with these works reveals them unlyrical to our frame of mind, disabused and laconic in style, brusque and idiosyncratic in their courses. Productions of a great creative talent, one of the few important composers this side the Atlantic, they remain rudimentary experiences; undeveloped in their two and three part contrapuntal technique; skirting monotony. But they speak; coldly, huskily, at first; then more persuasively. The bone-structure becomes flesh of authentic expressive values. Odd trains and orders grow logical and constructive.—A running fresco of sound, shy, lucid and austere. Evolved from the dances in Petrushka and Le Sacre, ballet-movements embody the green spirit of beginnings. The four episodes representing the four geological periods on the Aztec codices (world of water, wind, fire and lava, and earth), cast a sort of cosmic poem in aloof, incisive, distemper-like music: something of thin suns and sprouting sparse vegetation, bare, unbeguiled significations, and stiff motions of colts and things not long out of wintry cerements. In place of the blazonry, sensuality, and booze of the Russian music, we find an objective, aristocratic remoteness. The orchestra is small and sparsely used, contrapuntal in timbers as well as form. Gradually coming closer, never unbuttoning feeling, the music at last admits us into a strange kind of joy, childlike, ferocious, unfamiliar and still emancipatory. That, is Chavez's Aztec ballet The Four Suns.—And the sonata intensively continues the experience of objective form and virginal circumstance begun by the ballet. The bony, curiously unpronunciatory, unlyrical work, dry as a plant lost in sands, is even more difficult of access than The Four Suns. Its sparseness, trenchancy and architecturality, and the strictness of its time, are almost intolerable. The themes are at once innocent and precise, drumlike and decisively rhythmic: the treatment of the piano is essentially percussive. The four compact, boldly opposed little movements are predominantly staccato and martellato, moving with vigorous, resolute rhythms, jerky accents, and flinty sounds that appear to strike sparks from the anvil of the keyboard. Hollow octaves and single unsupported voices frequently appear; likewise instances of Chavez's favorite suspensions, brutal "deceptions" and interminations; while the impressionistic pedal is completely junked. At moments, as he plays it, you seem to hear modal, powerful, dissonant music executed as pupils of the French conservatory play their Bach: entirely from the precise finger tips. There is a certain tincture of archaic form: the third movement being a disguised fugue, and the preceding one having a scherzo-character. Still, neither of these movements are traditional. The scherzo-passage is a savage, dusty bit, one of the flighty rhapsodic movements in which Chavez lets us hear an atrocious echo of Aztec rattlings and

[278]

scratchings. And the fugue is bald, excessively compressed, and wry. Yet, gradually, some softness, color and flow, grow audible. Feeling begins to flow through the austere and cryptic stimulants; a little surprised at them and nonetheless grateful. We seem to be learning to extract serenity from sensations of hardness and iciness and angularity; to meet and control sadistic natural elements; commencing to draw water from the derisive rocks. It is dry, inclement and poor in the sublimation, the region of the spirit, to which we are introduced. Breath persists in coming hard, and there is not an abundance of objects able to gratify touch. None the less, something within is deeply grateful for and delighted with accommodation to a difficult nature. We have gained some new place, we know, elatedly.

It is no other than the shy, uncertain heart of the Mexican-American cosmos, the rocky, bare New World. To be sure, Chavez's music reflects something beside the new nature and spirit; something not experienced by himself. An amount of the spare, simple qualities of his pieces are incontrovertibly derived from eighteenth-century European classicism. But original aspects of his work are numerous, and preponderant; and these inexorable rhythms, pure severe contours, stony corners, crackling humors, rattlings, scrapings, arbitrary deceptions and withholdings, whipping dances of fire and of ice, make us feel America; particularly where she lies most herself in the high, dry mountainy spine of the continent, but to a degree in all her intraoceanic reaches. They catch marvelously simply the temper of life forced to adjust itself to her curiously cruel and splendid, profuse and irresponsive soil.—Stone, flint, little water, severe conditions, indistinct seasons on deserts and bare elephantine hills, vital need of impassivity.— Our intuition gets further corroboration in the composer's own personal consciousness. Were Chavez's waking interests unaccompanied by his musical performance, we might be at liberty to disregard his intense concern for the entire Mexican-American culture-situation. Particularly since so much curiosity of this kind, and intellectual orientation, has proven itself the expression of a mere wish-to-create, father of nothing. But the music overcomes the tendency to discount it. In the light of Chavez's piano-sonata and ballet, his great fresh knowledge of primitive Peruvian, Mexican, Amerindian music; his passion for the relics of Aztec culture as well as the forms of existing life;

and finally the rampant Pan-Americanism which
has led him to make his connections not with Paris
or Vienna, both of which bore him, but with New
York among its structural new-world marvels:
clearly appears the intellectual aspect of that fusion
between what is unconscious in the artist himself,
and what lies beyond him in the form of objective
nature.

An original classical music! What is its deed of
orientation but another assurance that the art which
Chavez brings us is such? Orientation toward a
new natural condition, a new society and soul,
is part, we know, of the function of every veritable
classicism. Since all art arises from the spirit of a
soil and a society in harmony with its soil, it tends
involuntarily to propagate the spirit that bore it;
whence the Atticism of so many Greek-enthusiasts.
And "classicism" is merely the quality of all first-
expressions of such new culture-worlds, invariably
"naïve" in Schiller's sense and little "sentimental"
in their youths; hence "objective," "architectural,"
"distemper-like" and "reserved" in their expressions. But, if we say, an original classical music, we
imply a Pan-American renaissance! The one is sign
of the other. An integral New World, based on the
embryonic one wrecked with the Aztecs!—Per-

haps we are a trifle late in our discovery, and
ungrateful toward a number of deserving North-
Americans? Orientations like Chavez's; identifica-
tions of what is in them and without them, have
been common to many of our recent writers. And
the soil, the unconscious, the community, have
spoken through painters as well as through poets.
Still, there is an excuse for our sudden exhilaration. We had thought the search for style limited
to the States. And here it comes, out of Latin
America; surely, sturdily paralleling that of our
best painters and poets; cheering us on with findings sympathetic to our own; assuring us of our
direction by mute evidence that that direction is
not sophistical and confined to a political state, but
the work of natural forces. Indeed, Chavez's music like Rivera's painting thrills us with the pros-
pect of the great rôle Mexico may play in the development of an American culture. It is not even
utterly fantastic to speculate on the possibility of a
leadership, in the harmonization of our western life
with the spirit of the soil, arising in the southern
republic. There was a culture in Mexico before the
Conquest, providing the little plant of the new
civilization a wall to grow against. We on the contrary possess no such ladder, our predecessors hav-

ing found little save barbarism before them. We don't, however, despair of our own republic; particularly since we have assurance that a Pan-American revival is indeed in progress, and that work from the rest of the hemisphere will shortly be coming to us, in ever greater quantity, as that of Chavez now: rendering us indifferent to anything except the problem in hand and life as we feel it; touching us anew with a spirit of an immense potentiality.

Gould naturalizes us on earth. To read his honest pagan poetry is to speed with the blood to the surface of the frame and feel breast-muscles expand among freely approachable and freely negligible objects. It is to be relaxed for direct, unhesitating expression; to find all loosened in ourselves and simply, fully, finally articulable; to go like old Roman statues come to life, forthright of port, ample of gesture, most proper earthlings. Gould's structures, whole poetic mechanism, is directed with the intensity, and swollen to the largeness, making us feel active and well. A corporeal rhythm

"Morning came to the gallop of great white stallions"

or

"And now for music. Play the phonograph!"

or

"Sing, nigger, in the distance"

establishes itself with each of his immediate first lines, grandly streaming, broad as a flag in a breeze.

[284]

Gould is none of your The Waste Land poets and bodiless heads, but the mind of a dense stately frame. What he projects are not cerebral periods synthesized from books and schematically put together, but rhythms superbly of a piece, automotive, having issue and inevitable suite. The best of his dithyrambic idyls and lyrics, Trilogy, Endymion and Moment Musicale are fairly intricate, capriciously varied and woven, fugal in form, full of refrains and recurrent motives and ideas; nonetheless steered steadily, pompously, toward their goals. They have the authority of the natural force. A curious mixture is blent in this Maine old Roman, massively at work in a style. Gould's slackness may recall Whitman's; but his accent is lighter and more urbane; and while his line is wearier than Whitman's, it is also shapelier and more musical, simultaneously epic and delicate. Evidently an ancient patrician raised by a New England schoolmarm, his gait and gesture are both proconsular, corpulent and majestic, and strangely elegant. His pitch and tone are equally complex; the one high, elevated and conversational at the same instant; the other orotund and playful, dreamy at times and chesty and exuberant at others; at moments drumlike with many round o's and a's; then as sibilant as the summer surf. Many of Gould's informal, shamelessly entertaining pieces are conversation poems, couched in spoken and familiar language necessarily stretched, weighted and intensified to express a precise and delicate as well as racy sensibility. If he can render the drunken Heracles, the instinctive Aphrodite and the athletes of Olympia robustly and earthily, he can also think and express himself with exactness and fluency of phrase; and let us feel an organism in the niceties and refinements, as well as in the broadnesses and emphases, of his language. Exceptional as they are; like the rhythm, pitch and tone remain certain and warm; sustained in their many playful or tragic, wistful or affirmative moods; golden with the unconscious conviction, integrity, making us recognize the will of nature.

Interior music of a man with a direct outlet, they carry us boldly into the world. One of Gould's earlier groups is called Murals. The title fits all his high-flown pieces, situated as they are on the objective plane of things, frontal and exterior in all their painfulness. Most happily they lack all "profundity," that trunk with the false bottom, built for purposes of concealment. The Gould poem is an impulse risen to the light and projected into the world as direct narrative, honest lyricism, clear pictiveness. Something of this happy exteriority is surely due its fugal refrains and repetitions, helping them to a mural, metope-like life. But more is due the extraverted imagery complementary to the broad corporeal rhythmicality. A potential Yankee Rubens, his brain awhirl with old Silenus and his fauns, flute-playing girls, and timbrel music; Gould, instead of the play of inner imitations through which so many moderns represent the world, gives us exuberant visual and auditory experiences; marshalling the objective world directly before us in a pompous pageant. Moment Musical shows us how

"three scarlet poppies by the garden path
  unfurled their flameous crepe, archly, elegantly, gra-
    ciously,
  as if to greet
  one who should come too late to find the rose.
  Luring, like shecats fawning, at high spring—
  gaudy, like painted paphians good to seek—
  languorous, flushed, like bacchantes reveling—
  they waited by the path as if to speak,
  as if to murmur things that women say—"

In "Laurels," that appetizing evocation of "the movement of lovely beings southward bound," the poet's "I" hears

"the clinking of innumerable stoppers to perfumery
      bottles,
the popping of innumerable corks and caps;
and together with the scent of Chypre, Cashmere Bou-
      quet, Narcisse de Chine,
there come to me wavering whiffs of Cognac, Wilson,
      Sterling, mountain dew, and of course hot gin,
all blending with the aromas of Helmar, Melachrino,
      Fatima.
There is an April shower of Hogarth lines, a blizzard
      of Chantilly, a typhoon of Hudnut."

At first, after the "buzzing, blooming" confusion
of so much contemporary metaphysical poetry,
with its simultaneous images in many sensory fields,
and entire ideality, Gould's may taste a trifle flat.
His imagery may appear too statemental, naming
things more often than substantiating them; at
least, leaving the realization to the rhythm and context. It is true he is sparing of tropes and figures.
Yet later, the baldness, the "few plain roses" of his
imagery recommends it. The pictures are faithful
to the concrete fact; the luminosity of day is about
them; a largeness, sumptuosity, holy animalism.
They are definite, the record of keen observation
and actual knowledge; and they are plentiful, and
abundant in contributory and structural items.
Besides, they are faithful to the concrete natural

fact of Gould's native New England, with its rivers, mill-towns, cupola'd white houses and old-fashioned gardens; this faithfulness crowding his earlier poems, particularly The Bard Sisters and Marnia, with pictures of what might be Portland, Gardiner, Augusta. Such an evocation of the spirit of place through a faithful record of selected aspects, in combination with the great broad rhythm and the symphonic manner, makes the commencement of Rosalind almost novelistic:

"On the Tague farm there was a rugged hill that
  looked on the Kennebec.
All the acclivities, save one, were bare of woods, and
  were barren as were the toplands also—
narrowing sweeps of bowldery pasturage rolling upward, rolling high, from sweeps of littoral mead-
  owland,
and useful only as grazing ground for the Tague
  sheep.
One acclivity, gutted deep by erosion, and glowering
  weirdly, inscrutably, on the Tague house, was
  even more barren than the others—
a vast and desolate claybank, furrowy, sterile, on
  which there grew not even the mullen, but on
  which, at midday, during the summer, the atmosphere was likely to dance in terpsichorean
  frenzy.

Another acclivity, one rising abruptly, and facing toward the river, was wooded with big oaks, big beeches, big pines, big birches, among which wound a sheep path, trodden firm, forever shady, with now a rustic gate, and with now a vista of meadow, of cornfield, of littoral boscage, or of the Kennebec itself, as discernible through a boscage.

The Tague house stood at the very brink of the river.

It was a large old gabled house, a colonial farmhouse with ramshackle sheds, which, joining one with another, and ranging one after another, connected the house with a great barn black with age.

In the dooryard there was an old neglected garden,— a garden in which there flourished, uncared for, the poppy, the rose, the heliotrope, the hollyhock, the sunflower, together with many a vine, and in which there spread about, unchecked, an undergrowth of pigweed.

At the end of the house, the end that faced toward the river, there were maples and oaks, with many a chokecherry tree, and a lone holly, together forming a spacious arbor in which there was fashioned a rustic settle, and in which one was tempted to linger, if only to listen to the wail of the catbird or the chatter of the squirrel, or to gaze on the swarthy Kennebec, at that point placid, and there curving about the hill, like the dusky arm of an erotic squaw.

[290]

The house stood a mile off from any other house.
In the sunny east parlor Rosalind lived, by herself."

Broad, imposing; yes, that is what Gould's images and his figures are; and broadness and largeness, and an innocent magnificence and animality
are their final attractiveness. The race will always
perforce entertain a greater sympathy for the scale
of beeves than that of sparrows; and Gould is anything but afraid of his own buffalo-like humanity.
His visual experiences and imagery are courage-
ously expanded to a stateliness recalling the high
renaissance's. It is invariably a "place of ruined pil-
lars" in Gould's tragedies, with a "sun immersed in
thoughts of his own splendor." The ocean

"a mighty warrior, slumbers, perhaps to prepare for
    the autumn combat—
slumbering lightly, however—
reclined at full length, suptine, naked, his head rest-
    ing in the lap of the doddering season, the hope-
    lessly fostering mother."

Here again is all the healthy "bad taste" of the
renaissance, all its ease among large appetites, spaces
and pomps; the ease of a deified humanity, its Christ

at the festive table among handsome sunburnt men, and beautiful women and children, and stuffs and wine and fruits. Indeed, Gould represents the sleeping Endymion in his cave on Latmos' side with a spirit of opulence and childlike definiteness that recalls a Veronese or a Rubens in his pagan riot:

"It is a spacious chamber, hidden from Helios, and forever dark,
save when Selene enters, lighting it, flooding it with the resplendence of white heat.
It is a silent place, with only the sound of the lover breathing, sometimes murmuring,
or of Selene cooing, gasping, chanting to the sound of the harp.

There are ceilings of cedar, the rafters inlaid with silver frets, and all upheld
by parian caryatides, titanic, bowed as with somnolescence, their feet
bracing against a parian floor, an ornate floor with border of anthemion,
and with a central mosaic, a Lesbian scene, all in lapis lazuli,
like the array of metopes flanked by the caryatides, all thus,
with scenes of bacchanalian rout and corybantian whirl.

[292]

At the back, between two caryatides, and hiding the
     lower part of a metope of Pan, squatting, per-
     chance to rest,
there stands an ebony bed, upholstered in celestial blue,
     and draped in such,
     and on this bed, itself raised on an ebony floor at
     the height of two low steps, their lifts inlaid
     with frets of silver,
Endymion lies, naked, his head resting in a silver cres-
     cent upholstered in the same celestial blue."

And like the grand inclusory rhythms and images, the significations salute the teeming earth and
all it bears. Gould's poems indeed initiate anew a
bodily comprehension of life, offering a grandiose
embrace to many elements which heads must find
irreconcilable. Having advisedly brought Whitman,
Rubens and Veronese into relation with this recent Yankee, let us here further connect him, com-
paratively unintegrated and unproductive as he
is, not alone to these demigods, but also to the old
heathen deities called Goethe and Tolstoy. A
pocketful of poems, neither masterly nor over-
whelming, his work none the less is of the stock of
theirs, born of an universal sympathy of the cloth
of their mighty ones. Gould's pieces too are "children of the sun," as their first, accurately definitive

title declared them; and their author, relatively inarticulate, and entangled by the world, fundamentally a "child of God and nature" like the Zeus of
Weimar and the individual compared by Maxim
Gorki to an old Russian divinity sitting under a
golden linden tree.* It appears that on our poet
too some early benediction had descended, letting
him love his own ego with the love simultaneously
embracing the world and the self; contenting him
in his timeless animal day indifferent to all "spirituality," moralism and rhetoric. Whole and
rounded bodies, men of his sort are necessarily all-
affirming spirits; sympathetic to all living; at home
in a world requiring no purpose, and giving everything its rights to existence. What they speak is
always an affirmation of "nature," man's animal,
always unregenerate being and all that is akin to
it. For it is only the head, the past, which rejects,
and discovers irreconcilables; and wars for exclusive
place. Contrariwise the body: product and kin of
many contending forces; and intuitively aware of
the universe's capacity for including the most antithetical, contradictory elements. It feels the
mighty transcending harmonies the head can never
comprehend. And in naïve recognition of their cor-

* See the recent essay by Thomas Mann in "Bemühungen."

[294]

poreality and profound sympathy with all action,
all life, even with death, the world has always
figured those who like Gould have uttered the
earthy, pagan knowledge not as spirits, but as
bodies: old heathen deities, old nature gods antedat-
ing dogmatic Christianity and living unregener-
ately on underneath its surface. Was not Goethe the
Zeus of Wiemar? And Tolstoy, the old Russian god
under the golden linden? Even Mozart stands in the
gardens of Salzburg an elegant naked Apollo wear-
ing the peruque of the eighteenth century. In very
profane, mythless America, Walt Whitman figures,
as a sort of hairy old weather-spirit half tree trunk
and half oracle. And Gould may possibly live on
in the imagination of his countrymen as a sort of
six foot satyr who was always tight, and wore few
draperies.

Implicitly, explicitly, multiply, the whole of
Gould's poetry echoes Whitman's homely, glorious
Lines to a Prostitute, most lowly reduction of the
universal affirmation and embrace common to the
entire crew. At first the recent New Englander's
affirmation of the pan-life, and "not till the sun
excludes you, do I exclude you" falls principally
into the form of a passionate embrace of passion
itself. That was inevitable, since Gould is a New

England puritan; and Puritanism's fear of life and the senses, and consequent cerebralism, is finally a fear of the propensities. Rosalind, Marnia, and the other pictures of New England life bring us to a pause before the great red rose not at all in easy rapture, and in a mixture of sheer wonder and constricting anguish, tenderness and sorrow, that resembles the ardent state's. We find the flower growing in dark gardens, for this is the land of the Androscoggin. It has sudden tragic blossomings. Yet the wondrous pathos with which Gould illumines it alone would prove him a poet: creature who knows that impermanent and connected with death as it is, its color and shape and scent are worth all hoarded powers; even fame and the making of poems. Scarce another American has made us feel as deeply and as chastely the ineffable moment of its blossoming. Later, Gould's appreciation of passion turns into the appreciation of all vital diversion and exercise, culminating in the tragic Trilogy * with a glorification of heroic action; and *"salut au monde"* reverberates more directly from his verse. To be sure, its volume and heartiness are not Whitman's: Gould is a younger brother of the affirmative tribe. A certain weariness in his rhythms

* Published in The Second American Caravan.

and tenuity in his productions has been mentioned; the deficiency takes the form of an overmeasure of pain and sorrowfulness in the significations. For all his poems' directness and broadness of advance, grand as the swing of stallions, there is some feeling of constriction in this universe. The flesh has been wounded. The dances have the corybantic whirl of death. Life is a closing book, its grandest pages past. The touch of resignation is particularly prominent in Murals, in Endymion, in the marvelously lyrical Moment Musicale and several others of a group possibly pendant to the experiences celebrated in The Bard Sisters and Marnia. The first of these poems seems to be an expression of the fate inherent in physical possession; Endymion gives us an unforgettable picture of a man forever asleep in all his youth, in the side of a mountain visited only by the moon. And in the last the speaker recognizes in the eyes into which he is gazing

> "Something of a wreck that lies
> too deep for salvage or recovery,
> a treasure-ship once laden to the prow
> with old choice wines, rich fabrics, and a host
> of rare diaphanous gems, but riding low—
> too low, and doomed to end among the lost.
> Perchance it foundered in a peaceful swell—

rudder and sail neglected for long dreams.
Or in a stormy trough, when lightning fell,
too quickly sundering the straining beams.
I wished that it had drifted, to this day.
I wish that it were yet to drift my way."

Frantically, it calls him to seize the last escaping
minute:

"Strum the guitar.
I want no more of what men call their faith.
I want no more of what men call their hope.
Strum the guitar.
I want diversion—
a sustenance for the beggared hours, famished,
        dying, tottering off to die;
not that a few may be revived thus; no—
but that they shall not perish as they go.
I loathe dead hours."

What began as mandolin music has been known
to grow unaccountably full and orchestral. Certainly, there is nothing tinny and tinkling in those
of Gould's poems in which the simultaneous embrace of the body's ephemeral life and of the common, close reality, finally becomes ample and intense. Aphrodite, Laurels, Ars Longa, Vita Brevis,
Postscript and Night-Songs are playful enough in
tone and subject; but it would be unpardonably

naïve not to recognize in their "heiterkeit" the seriousness of an ethic, the ideal of health, plenitude and euphoria. Ostensibly a mere rehandling of amusing old myths, Aphrodite is indeed a very sharp, reverend discovery of instinctive femininity. Laurels, gay rhapsody and luxurious fancy about the yearly southward migration of courtesans, actually hymns the earthly nutriments, the innocent silks and cognacs there for the appreciative sense. Through an old Greek head in the Metropolitan Museum of Art, we learn of a sharp and likeable fellow—wily,—agile—his spring that of a panther —a lover, a wit, a gentleman, a pleasing liar,

"ready for a night with the Hetairai, ready for a day with the runners, ready for death at Thermopylæ."

Postcript (to a letter to Wallace Stevens) is a most pleasant poem about the author's cats; yet between the whimsical lines we hear again, lightly perhaps but clearly, the grand burden of all the men of Gould's glad type: aversion from other-worldliness, dreams of paradise and golden ages past and future; and joyous, full, acceptation of the perilous, ephemeral moment, the here, the now, on the very brink of death, as man's only good and possession. This, Gould's master-idea and perhaps life-long attribute, gets its tragic, sonorous expression in the grand epic manner of Trilogy, his latest, most significant and probably most representative work. Between choral battle pieces the poem represents the three Athenian tragi-dramatists; makes three poets triumphant in their works and sure of enduring fame, say what they know of life. And each speaks of Salamis: Æschylus who fought there, Sophocles who danced there, and Euripides who was born there; and each looks backward with passion to that glorious moment, hour of highest diversion, sunburst of human enthusiasm and liberty. They have lived after, written their tragedies and had ephemeral triumphs. And all living-after has been bitter; and each says "Would I had died at Salamis!" The soldier's death, then, the death of the fighter, the lover, the agonist of life and freedom, rather than all the immortal masterpieces, the laurels of the mob, the memory of mankind! Die and be:

"Und so lang du das nicht hast
Dieses: Stirb und werde!
Bist du nur ein trüber Gast
Auf der dunklen Erde."

Wallace Gould to-day stands the most interesting force among the many brilliant rivaling presences of American poetry; holding that eminence despite the incompleteness of his work. As the author of Trilogy he offers to bring Whitman's bodily, cosmic affirmation to a new flood in verse; even though by the side of his great prototype's, his epic measures remain relatively tenuous. Proclaimed by every one of his gestures, and by the rhythm and form of his best pieces one of the heroic brood, Gould is scarcely yet the full-grown figure; and while Trilogy expresses a maturity and large experience of life, and roars with force, the balance of the poems collected in his forthcoming volume, broad in their attacks and positive in their tones as they are, lack the great accent. His artistic personality remains a little special; and comprehensive as it is, its expressions are too limited in character, playing too small a range of notes and embodying too few experiences, to be universally eloquent. One cannot be content with his Greek recapitulation, free of local color though they be. And his poems are not the work of a few years! Several of them appeared in the Seven Arts, and in the Little Review during the time of its honesty: Gould's discovery having resulted from one of Marsden Hartley's forays way down east. Still, for all his slowness, we find this singer more promissory at present than T. S. Eliot, E. E. Cummings, Hart Crane, Marianne Moore and several other of the poets whose muses still hold out hope of issue; distinguished as most of these personalities are, and superior to Gould in several points of art. Line for line, Eliot's and Cummings', Crane's and Marianne Moore's poetry surpasses his, as line for line, the poetry of Webster surpasses that of Mr. W. S. They too have read everything. And their use of words is more advanced, daring and virtuosic than Gould's. As absolutist poets, they stand high on the hill of expression. Nonethless, they stand there in partial incompletude; all of them, even Hart Crane, the most passionate of the group, essentially divided; finders of head-rhythms wanting the great logic: Eliot with resignation; Cummings with the frantic revolt that makes his poetry the extraordinary attempt of an analytic faculty to imitate and grasp the body's integral, spontaneous, incomprehensible drunkenness. That integral, spontaneous, elusive warmth and combustability Gould however possesses; naturalizing us on earth by virtue of it; and filling us with hope of him. Affirmation of man's whole nature, embrace of all the earth bound up with it, "salut au monde" indeed, is the American principle. Presently not only

in the idea of the American democracy but in all
vigorous American thought, it must come to us out
of the air, the soil, the climate as well as institu-
tionally, since it is so deeply ingrained in us from
birth. If there is a green American tradition, it is
this. The dreams of all our moral authorities from
Emerson to Randolph Bourne have embodied it.
The grandest of our expressions, Lincoln and Whitman's of yesterday, Stieglitz's of to-day, have projected it into the sky like a star, and given us feet
and hearts to move toward it. There has been no
major American life uninspired of it. No wonder
then that we should recognize in Wallace Gould,
setting us in the way of the old, the great American
adventure, the voice of the country too long silent
in its verse; happily reawakening.

WHY DO I WRITE? *

THE question delights me. Without exaggeration
I may say that it draws heaven closer. Though I do
not know the answer, I am certain of the direction
in which the solution to this and related problems
is to be found; and that, believe me, is quite trans-
porting.— Seriously: I write "because" of a sympathetic relationship existing between myself and
something invisible and unknown to me, enveloping me like a living atmosphere and moving within
me like my blood. This curious oceanic substance
fascinates and solicits me incessantly; and might,
as a steady object of interest, be called the cause
of the activity directed toward it. Always ranging
somewhere upon its borders, I feel it close behind
things that are known to me, man-made as well as
natural things, buildings and streets and works of
art as well as faces and bodies, land- and cloud-
scapes. Frequently I find it connected with the past
and the future, particularly my past and that of the
city of New York; sometimes with my parents;
more often with a slowly growing, changing group

* An answer to the questionaire of the authors of On Parade.

[304]

of intimates, collaborators and acquaintances; with books, painting and music; and with a number of concepts and interests. Though I feel it initial to a degree in or behind everything; that degree is never very large and infectious in certain classes of work, on later examination proving themselves consequences of precepts, theories, conscious principles and all other kinds of personal interests. Only things done in sympathy with the strange, unpredictable, unfathomable states of this ever-changing "unknown" invisible element; in disregard of the habits of the past and the convictions of authorities; and in unsanctified fields and by unhallowed methods, succeed in moving me; particularly those responsive to the latency pressing directly upon me and my time. There, as in many natural forms, its presence or trace is a sort of wonder, a thing of delight and fine torment arousing curiosity; spurring me in spite of the fact that I know I can never seize or possess it, to search out the source of agitation; at least, to try and push back a little the mists shrouding it from me. There is nothing more rewarding than exploration of its ineffable reaches; all my profound pleasures containing some such element of search, and part sensuous, part intellectual discovery in it. To touch even the fringe of its garment is to feel everything made right, to find, in the words of Blake "one thought filling immensity." Not the least of its great attractions is just the fact that for all I may get at, not one thousandth part of it will be revealed to me before I die.

—And why do my discoveries tend to take what, with no mean charity, might be called "artistic" form? Why do they come associated with words and pressing for verbal expression? And why do I try to make words render the very material feel of things? The answers to these riddles lie very close to the "reason" for my desire to discover. I am convinced that were a complete physiological analysis of myself and of the society in which I grew up, at all possible (and for the present the complete analysis of a person and society are out of the question) these matters would still remain dark. Final answers are much further up the road than any of us have gotten. Hence, although I can mention a few so-called hereditary factors, I do so without protestation.—Among the six individuals my grandfathers and great-grandfathers, there were four professional-men: a doctor, a school-master, a cantor and a banker. The remaining two were brewers; but possibly they too, facilitated a

little non-commercial career. There was marked
æstheticism and even intellectuality in both my
parents. I grew up amid an amount of spontaneous
music-making: my mother being a talented pianist;
and amid much talk of books and writers: my father being an indefatigable reader, chiefly of Dick-
ens's novels and the histories of Gibbon, Macau-
lay, Schiller, Taine and others.—My own absorption in literature commenced somewhere around
my twelfth year. During the winter following my
mother's death, my father read me the trial scene
from Ivanhoe: I felt the intense emotion in his
voice. One day I discovered the historical romance
in the school lending-library; and though I had
devoured the usual Alger, Oliver Optic and Henty,
realized that I had come upon a new and intenser
pleasure. I must have read Ivanhoe fifteen times
during the next two or three years; and Anne of
Geierstein many times also. I had already found
"writing," fun; and about the time of the Scott
craze was occupied in forming a publishing house
with the aid of my cousin Henry Furst. That is,
Henry and I wrote "books" which we pinned together, and lent to each other.—In the fall of my
fifteenth year, I found Alexander's Feast, An Ode
for Saint Cecilia's Day and The Eve of Saint Ag-

nes in an old anthology: it was a little as though someone had poured the contents of jewel-boxes over my dizzied head. Later, Shelley (to whom I had been attracted by a word concerning his atheism), George Meredith, Whitman, Morris, Pater and Yeats became the conjurers. I remark that all these prosemen and poets belong to the high-stylistic company (the Yeats who interested me was the earlier, pre-raphaelite one). However, I suspect that the authors who set an ideal before me first were George Moore and Arthur Symons, the Moore of the confessions and Evelyn Innes, the Symons of the essays and Spiritual Adventures; all of them read during my sophomore year at college. Here, particularly in the Moore, was something shiningly "real," racy, magical of phrase, sensuously delicious, and close to what I felt mysteriously affecting in gray evenings and moments when lights and houses sped by rainy train-windows. It must have been a little before this time that I knew quite definitely that I expected to "write." Now, I see that the decision had been made a long time before, and had been sitting there quietly like someone in a railway waiting-room attending his train-hour. While at prep-school, I had loosely spoken of becoming a chemist, a forester, and even a lawyer. When I was small, my father had persuaded me that I was to become a doctor like his own good parent. But I had always spoken without enthusiasm, under some exterior compulsion.—This final circumstance, like those preceding it, I cite merely as straws and twigs revealing the way a current moved.—I hope to be able to push further along this line, on some not too remote occasion.